Spiritual Warfare

Stanley Smith

Spiritual WARFARE

First published by Spirit Publications, 2006
Author House, 2010

ISBN: 978-1-4490-0356-2 (sc)
ISBN: 978-1-4490-0355-5 (e)

Printed in the United States of America
Bloomington, Indiana

AuthorHouse™
1663 Liberty Drive
Bloomington, IN 47403
www.authorhouse.com
Phone: 1-800-839-8640

Spirit Publications

E-mail: *warfareevangelist@yahoo.com*

Spiritual WARFARE
Contents

Introduction
Spiritual Warfare

Introduction
Spiritual Warfare

There are many great books on Spiritual Warfare. Receive this work as an addition and complement to the other Spiritual Warfare works.

Many of us have not yet pictured the Lord as the leader of a great army. The Lord is called The Lord of Host (The Lord of an Army). He is a God of War. Exodus 15:3 declares, the Lord is a man of War; the Lord is his name.

Spiritual Warfare is the confrontation between the Kingdom of God and the kingdom of darkness. Everyone that is born into the Kingdom of God is part of this warfare and should actively participate. We are God's children, filled with His Spirit. He has commissioned us through His Word to wage war. All Holy Ghost filled Christians must recognize that resisting the devil, casting out devils and intercession are not special ministries set aside for just the deliverance minister, but to them that believe.

We cannot rid the elements of demons, powers and principalities. We can't send them to prison. Demons are spirits. Those used by God in warfare should teach, train and lead the charge. We should teach people how to engage in warfare, live free and break the grip of the enemy.

When Jesus Christ was baptized and received the Holy Ghost, he went into the wilderness, he fasted forty days and was tempted by Satan. Jesus defeats Satan's attack with the Word of God. The Scriptures report that after John the Baptist went to prison, Jesus came into Galilee, preaching the Gospel of the Kingdom of God. Scripture Reference Mark 1:9-15

The first miracle Jesus did was turn water into wine, John 2:1-12. The second miracle was casting out demons, Mark 1:23. Witnesses were amazed and confounded! Mark 1:27...What thing is this? What new doctrine is this? For with authority commandeth he even the unclean spirits, and they do obey him.

Never before in the earthly realm; neither is it recorded in scripture, any account of any person of God, patriarch, prophet, prophetess or judge— casting out a demon spirit. The Kingdom of God with all its majesty, authority, dominion and power was truly at hand. The King of Kings was preaching about His Kingdom, yet he did not come as a King. He made himself of no reputation and came as a man in the form of a servant.

The Good News is the Gospel of the Kingdom. 1 Corinthians 4:20...The kingdom of God is not in word, but in power. Jesus preached about His Kingdom then demonstrated the power of His Kingdom.

In the kingdom of God we have access to all of the Kingdom benefits. We have forgiveness of our sins, healing for all of our diseases, God's mercy and everything contained in the promises of God.

In Matthew 10:1-8 After a season of teaching and demonstrating, the Lord sends the disciples to preach and demonstrate the power of the Kingdom of God. Matthew 10:1...And when he had called unto him his twelve disciples, he gave them power against unclean spirits, to cast them out, and to heal all manner of sickness and all manner of disease. Verses 7-8...As ye go, preach, saying, The kingdom of heaven is at hand. Heal the sick, cleanse the lepers, raise the dead, cast out devils: freely ye have received, freely give.

Intercession/Prayer, Casting Out Devils, Worship, Giving, Preaching and the Practice of God's Word are all methods of conducting Spiritual Warfare.

In the Book of Mark alone, there are 18 references to Spiritual Warfare/Casting Out Devils. See page 81, Casting Out Devils. We are to be active in Spiritual Warfare defensely and offensely. It is a short Gospel that just talks about the who and the what and does not tell us the why, nor demonstrates the how.

We know that everything is not a demon. Scripture does support that demons affect the weather and cause sickness and disease. Peoples attitudes, behavior, values and beliefs are affected by demons in a negative way.

Ephesians 6:18
Praying always with all prayer and supplication
in the Spirit, and watching thereunto with all
perserverance and supplication for all saints.

Warfare
Intercessor
Part 1

Your praying
is Praying in
the Holy Ghost,
to bombard Heaven
with Top Secret Spiritual
Communications, petitions
and supplications on behalf
of the church and others,
loosening the grip, breaking
down the blockades and
destroying the strategies of
the Adversary. Your intercession
delivers globally (as some sleep);
requesting, transporting and
directing supernatural help,
and Ministering in the Holy
Ghost where distance
and time are subject
to the Spirit.

Dedication

To the Intercessory Prayer Warriors
across the world, whose ministry it is
to pray without ceasing.

I take this time to thank you and say that
you have been directed by God to bend your
knees. You are directed by God to pray
before trouble comes, while trouble is
present and when trouble has gone.
Intercessors, you are the unseen essential
ministry of the body of Jesus Christ
and great shall be your reward.

Chapter 1
Prayer

Prayer can be called the long range weapon similar to a spear or javelin. There is no distance in prayer for the warfare intercessor. In The Desert Storm War a new missile was used. The missile was armed with new technology and intelligence. These missiles travelled great distances with pinpoint accuracy, virtually undetected until impact. Wow! Doesn't this sound like intercessory prayer.

We can attack the enemy in prayer for situations around the globe. He won't see us or hear us until the anointing makes impact and breaks the yoke. We can speak the word and get results in battles, not in our immediate physical presence. We need to pray and understand our authority in prayer. We are not lowly worms, but we are covenant children of God who are right now seated in heavenly places, far above principality and power, Ephesians 1:19-21. We have to understand our standing: a position of right relationship with Christ.

There is no distance in prayer when we speak and pray in faith. The Centurion said to Jesus in Matthew 8:5-8...Lord my servant lieth at home sick of the palsy, grievously tormented. Jesus said, I will come and heal him. The centurion answered and said, Lord, I am not worthy that thou shouldest come under my roof: but speak the word only, and my servant shall be healed...Verse 13 and his servant was healed in the selfsame hour. The centurion understood the authority that Christ had when his orders were spoken. Speak it, pray it, it will come to pass!

The scripture constrains us to be ever prayerful Luke 18:1...men ought to always to pray, and not to faint...

Ephesians 6:18...Praying always with all prayer and supplication in the Spirit, and watching thereunto with all perseverance and supplication for all saints.

1 Thessalonians 5:17...Pray without ceasing.

1 Timothy 2:1...I Exhort, therefore, that first of all, supplications, prayers, intercessions, and giving of thanks, be made for all men.

Remembering this...

2 Corinthians 10:4...For the weapons of our warfare are not carnal, but mighty though God to the pulling down of strongholds.

We exercise great power in prayer. Make war through intercessory prayer. Your intercession can touch lives, locally, regionally, nationally, internationally, and universally.

What does it mean to Pray/to Intercede?

To pray is to make a request unto God for ourselves, family, or others. Intercession-the act of prayer and/or pleading on behalf of another; a technical term for approaching a King. Many preach that nothing is done on earth but by prayer; a request of man. The Prophet Daniel is a model person of prayer. Daniel 6:10...he kneeled upon his knees three times a day, and prayed, and gave thanks before his God, as he did aforetime.

These are some things that hinder our prayers from being answered:

(1) unbelief-James 1:6...Let him ask in faith nothing wavering. Romans 14:23...for whatever is not of faith is sin.

(2) fear-Isaiah 35:4...Say to them that are of a fearful heart, Be strong, fear not; behold, your God will come with vengeance, even God with a recompense; he will come and save you.

(3) marital disharmony-1 Peter 3:7...In like manner, ye husbands, dwell with them according to knowledge, giving honor unto the wife, as unto the

weaker vessel, and as being heirs together of the grace of life, that your prayers be not hindered.

(4) unforgiveness-Matthew 6:15...But if you forgive not men their trespasses, neither will your Father forgive your trespasses.

(5) asking amiss-James 4:3...Ye ask, and receive not, because you ask amiss, that ye may consume it upon your lusts. (Amiss means to ask inappropriately).

(6) demonic resistance-Daniel 10:12-13...Then said he unto me, Fear not, Daniel: for from the first day that thou didst set thine heart to understand, and to chasten thyself before thy God, thy words were heard, and I am come for thy words. But the prince of the kingdom of Persia withstood me one and twenty days: but, lo, Michael, one of the chief princes, came to help me; and I remained there with the kings of Persia.

(7) unrepented sin-Mark 11:25...And when ye stand praying, forgive. Psalms 66:18...If I regard iniquity in my heart, the Lord will not hear me. 19...But verily God hath heard me; he hath attended to the voice of my prayer. The prerequisite for answered prayer is coming correctly, asking as scripture teaches.

Chapter 2
The Lord's Prayer-
The Instruction in Prayer

Luke 11:1-4...Lord teach us how to pray.

Matthew 6:9-13 is called The Lord's Prayer. These verses are actually the instructions Jesus gives after his disciples requested, Lord teach us how to pray, Luke 11:1-4. We will still refer to these verses as The Lord's Prayer.

The instruction...Matthew 6:9 After this manner, therefore, pray ye:

Matthew 6:9...Our Father-Instructs us to whom to direct our prayers to. Isaiah 9:6...His name shall be called The Mighty God, The Everlasting Father. Jesus instructs again in prayer. John 16:23-And in that day ye shall ask me nothing. Verily, verily, I say unto you, Whatsoever ye shall ask the Father in my name, he will give it you.

Matthew 6:9...Which art in Heaven-Instructs us where to direct our prayers. Isaiah 66:1 Declares, The heaven is my throne, and the earth is my footstool. God's seat of power or throne of power is in the heavens far above the earth. His headship is far above the earth.

Matthew 6:9...Hallowed be thy name-Remember whose help we are requesting: the King of Kings, and Lord of Lords, the Alpha and Omega, The Beginning and End, The First and The Last. Give the highest regard and acknowledgment of His Name. We are approaching the throne of the King! Psalms 95:6...oh come, let us worship and bow down: let us kneel before the Lord our maker. Exalt the Lord our God and worship at his footstool; for he is holy.

Matthew 6:10...Thy Kingdom Come-Lord let your government be in control. I submit myself to your Lordship. Thy Kingdom Come—your kingdom of prosperity, your kingdom of healing, your kingdom of salvation, your kingdom of deliverance, your eternal kingdom, and your kingdom of righteousness. Psalms 103:19...The Lord hath prepared his throne in the heavens; and his kingdom ruleth over all.

Matthew 6:10...Thy will be done in earth, as it is in Heaven-Pray that the ways, purposes and practices of Heaven be present in the earth as it is in Heaven. Psalms 18:30...As for God, his way is perfect.

Spiritual Warfare

Matthew 6:11...Give us this day our daily bread.
Matthew 7:7...Ask, and it shall be given you...We
are to ask for daily provision of food, clothing
and our physical necessities. Also, we are to
ask for our daily spiritual bread—a daily word.
Matthew 4:4... Man shall not live by bread alone,
but by every word that proceedeth out of the
mouth of God. We are to live in faith day by day.
Deuteronomy 8:2-4...God reminds the Israelites
how he daily supplied their food, water, raiment,
shoes, health and protection for forty years.
He wants to supply our daily needs and he will.
Just ask Him.

Matthew 6:12...And forgive us our debts, as we
forgive our debtors. We must have a right heart
towards others if we expect the same from God.
Matthew 6:14-15...For if ye forgive men their
trespasses, your heavenly Father will also forgive
you: but if ye forgive not men their trespasses,
neither will your Father forgive your trespasses.
God expects us to show the same love and forgiveness toward others that we request from him. Our
hearts must be pure if we are expecting God to
answer us.

Matthew 6:13...And lead us not into temptation, but
deliver us from evil. One translation says...and let
us not be put to the test and/or subject us not to
testing, but keep us free from the evil one. The

word declares in Jeremiah 1:8...I am with thee to deliver thee, saith the Lord. Pray that the Lord keeps us from temptation and the evil one. This instruction finishes with a doxology: a formulated prayer or worship. Scholars say the following words are not included in original manuscripts; yet we will continue.

Matthew 6:13...For thine is the kingdom, and the power, and the glory, forever. Amen. Psalms 22:28...For the Kingdom is the Lord's: and he is the Governor among the nations. Romans 13:1... For there is no power but of God. Daniel 7:14... And there was given him dominion, and glory, and a kingdom...and his kingdom that which shall not be destroyed. Amen!

Jude (verse 25) To the only wise God our Savior, be glory and majesty, dominion and power, both now and for ever. Amen!

Testimony

During my early life we lived in a Coal Mining town of Maben, West Virginia. The blacks lived in a segregated part of the town closer to the mines. There were two church groups—a Baptist Group and a Holiness Group. We shared the one church building. We were the Holiness Group—Holy Ghost filled tongue talkers, baptized in the name of Jesus Christ. The Baptist had service and Sunday School first. We had the second service and a weekly night service. Our pastor was Pastor Robert Love. He was a very nice man whose daughter was my godmother.

I remember going to his house playing, eating and sitting on his lap. He would pray and utter blessings over my sisters and me regularly. As a young child, I remember going to church to prayer and worship service. I remember riding through the hills of West Virginia to other prayer meetings. I was a sick child and the mothers would pick me up in their arms and lay me on the altar and pray over me. I used to hate it. I remember walking to Sunday School at still another church and always being first so I could ring the bell; the call to prayer and worship. I saw my mother, a young wife, pray and weep in prayer. I remember seeing my father in prayer with a preacher before he was baptized.

I was sick with asthma and Mama would pray over me. Daddy would hold me sometimes and pray, give me my medicine, and prop me up in the old rocking chair for the night. The medicine didn't help. It would just put me to sleep. My Mama always prayed for me and for my condition.

One day, as God would have it, Mama passed by a church of a Jewish preacher in Mullens, West Virginia. He had a sign up that read "come get a prayer cloth," Acts 19:11. Mama got a prayer cloth and pinned it to my clothes. As God ordained my healing, by his stripes, I was healed. So healed was I that I played on three championship teams in junior high, lettered three years in high school and was a West Virginia State finalist in track and field in two events.

I am still healed and have been healed of other ailments in Jesus' name and I am writing this testimony these 40 years later. Hallelujah! As a product of God's mercy and healing through this preacher, as a minister I give out prayer cloths regularly. Acts 19:11-12.

Testimony

When I came to Washington, DC, I became a police officer. While working one Sunday morning, I was chasing a man who had left the scene of an accident. I chased him and after tackling him, we fought. He got my gun from my holster and was yelling over and over, "I'm going to kill you". I began to pray and saw my life flash before me. I said, "Lord please don't let me die like this in this alley." I prayed Lord give me another chance and I will serve you. At the time there were other officers in the area trying to find me.

I said, "Lord I promise." Immediately help came from every direction. God gave me another chance. I was so outdone by the experience, I would not charge the man with the assault. I asked him why he wanted to kill me. He said he had spent 9 years in jail and was afraid he would be sent back. He said I would have killed you and began to weep bitterly. I charged him with some tickets and told him to go to court and pay them, and there would be no other charges. He did. My Sergeant and Lieutenant did not understand. God gave me a second chance and I gave the brother another chance.

Two days later still very stunned from the fact I came so close to dying without God for the third time, I went to the bookstore at a nearby mall and bought a Bible and began to read it. I read day and night. After work I read the word. I was asked again at work, why did I let the man go. I called my mother and asked questions. She asked was anything wrong. I said, "No ma'am, I just need some answers."

After hearing the preaching of Bishop Ralph E. Green, I was baptized in the name of Jesus Christ and received the baptism of the Holy Ghost.

I am glad I prayed and I am glad the Lord had somebody somewhere praying for me. I remember calling Mama and saying, "Mama, I received the Holy Ghost." Mama was rejoicing over the phone. "Praise God. He heard my prayer".

Yes, prayer moves the hand of God. Prayer changes things.

Chapter 3
The Intercessors

Daniel 6:10...he kneeled upon his knees three
times a day, and prayed, and gave thanks
before his God, as he did aforetime.

In the early scriptures, the most revealing
account of the Warfare Prayer is in the
Book of Daniel. Daniel was the Prophet who
interpreted dreams, the Ruler and the Prayer
Intercessor. Daniel was a man who prayed three
times a day, prayed in season and out. Is prayer
seasonal? Some Christians only pray when there
is a season of personal trouble. Daniel prayed
daily unto God. Daniel 6:1-10...Daniel prayed; even
after all the rulers conspired against him and had a
law drafted that anyone petitioning any god or man
except the king would be thrown into a den of lions.
He yet prayed to the Almighty God. He was not
afraid. He did not waiver.

Daniel 6:10...Now when Daniel knew that the writing was signed, he went into his house; and his windows being open in his chamber toward Jerusalem, he kneeled upon his knees three times a day, and prayed, and gave thanks before his God, as he did aforetime. Daniel 6:11...Then these men assembled, and found Daniel praying and making supplication before his God. The King was bound by his own law and Daniel was thrown into the den of lions. Strangely, the King speaks a word, Daniel 6:16... The God, whom thou servest continually, he will deliver thee.

Darius the King knew that Daniel was faithful and relentless in his service to the Almighty God. He knew God was faithful to Daniel. Daniel was also faithful in his service to King Darius as long as it did not violate his relationship with God.

Daniel 6:19...Then the king rose up early in the morning, and went in haste unto the den of lions to check and see if God had delivered Daniel. Listen to Daniels response. Daniel 6:22...My God hath sent his angel, and hath shut the lions' mouths, that they have not hurt me... and a portion of verse 23...and no manner of hurt was found upon him, because he believed in his God. Darius even wrote a decree concerning Daniel and his God, read Daniel 6:25-28.

Daniel's daily commitment to pray fortified his faith in God. Daniel was covered by his prayers and through his relationship with God. In the New Testament, Luke 18:1 (Jesus declares)...that men ought always to pray and not to faint.

Daniel had grace and instruction from God concerning the burden of praying for the entire nation of Israel, while fulfilling his service to an earthly King. In Daniel 9:1-22...Daniel is interceding for Israel. Daniel did not pray the same prayers everyday. Through his intimacy with God, he experienced the joy of prayer, praying prayers filled with life and power. He asks forgiveness for the transgressions of Israel. Daniel 9:3-4...And I set my face unto the Lord God, to seek by prayer and supplications, with fasting, and sackcloth and ashes: And I prayed unto the Lord my God, and made my confession...And look at what happened in Daniel 9:21:

Daniel 9:21...Yea, whiles I was speaking in prayer, even the man Gabriel, whom I had seen in the vision at the beginning, being caused to fly swiftly, touched me about the time of the evening obla-tion, Verse 22...And he informed me, and talked with me, and said, O Daniel, I now come forth to give thee skill and understanding. God sent his angel as Daniel was praying. God is surely awesome! Daniel is among those Bible people who prayed and God sent an angel to bring a swift answer and to give understanding.

Daniel was a man for all seasons. He was steadfast in prayer unto God. In Daniel the 10th chapter, there is a description of war between the Kingdom of God—God's angels and the kingdom of darkness—Satan's angels. Daniel 10:2 Daniel says that he was in mourning three full weeks. He was in prayer and fasting for three weeks. At the end Daniel has a vision. He is told that from the first day his words/prayer were heard, yet the answer sent through an angel was withstood or hindered/delayed by the prince of the kingdom of Persia, a principality spirit. And Michael one of God's Chief Princes came and helped the angel. The angel told Daniel that he came to help him understand what should befall his people in the latter days.

The Book of Daniel is a Prophetic History of the earth and mankind's past, present, and future. The Book of Revelation is the conclusion of what was given in the Book of Daniel. These Books give insight about the Kingdoms of the Earth, the kingdom of darkness and the Ministry of the Lord Jesus Christ and the Salvation of all of His saints and their eternal abode in Christ.

Paul gives a similar decree to Timothy concerning prayer; 1 Timothy 2:1-2...I exhort therefore, that, first of all, supplications, prayers, intercessions, and giving of thanks, be made for all men. For kings, and for all that are in authority, that we may lead a quiet and peaceable life in all godliness and honesty.

The Warfare Intercessor is one who prays on behalf of others. Many people are trying to get around praying or replacing prayer with something else. Nothing can replace prayer. Remember the person or group being prayed for, may not be able to pray with any effectiveness nor has a mind to pray. We, the church, must pray in the Spirit, praying in tongues, so that the Holy Ghost will help us to pray as we ought. Romans 8:26...Likewise the Spirit also helpeth our infirmities: for we know not what we should pray for as we ought: but the Spirit itself maketh intercession for us with groanings which cannot be uttered. Verse 27...And he that searcheth the hearts knoweth what is the mind of the Spirit, because he maketh intercession for the saints according to the will of God.

There is a Great Church in Seoul, Korea where the people of God pray in shifts at a place called Prayer Mountain. What a grand and wonderful report!

Warfare Intercession is serious business. We must be dedicated, diligent, relentless and on our Warfare Praying Post. We all are called to pray. Many must excel in prayer and become Warfare Intercessors.

Let us look at Warfare Intercession in the New Testament. In the Book of Acts in the twelfth chapter verse 1. Herod the King stretched forth his hands to vex certain of the church. Verse 2...And he killed James the brother of John, with the sword. Verse 3...And because he saw it pleased the Jews, he proceeded further to take Peter also. (Then were the days of unleavened bread). Herod planned to kill Peter and his death was postponed because of the Passover. Look at how the church responded. Acts 12:5...Peter, therefore, was kept in prison: but prayer was made without ceasing of the church unto God for him!

The prayer made without ceasing until God answered, was intercession for Peter.

In Acts 12:5-19...Peter was on death row. We must understand that because of love, through grace and in faith, we are dutiful in prayer. Someone somewhere needs your prayers. Peter needed the urgent prayers of the church. The church prayed without ceasing and our God answered mightily. Look at the delivering power of God! Peter was bound with chains and an angel came and took Peter from between two guards. The angel led Peter past the first and the second guards to gates that opened of their own accord into the street.

Once in the street Peter realized he was not dreaming, but that he had been delivered by God through the prayers of the saints. Peter went to the house where the saints were praying. This is a second account of prayer being made and the Lord sending an angel to help.

Peter needed help and when help came at first, Peter found it hard to believe what was actually happening. The saints were praying for his deliverance and when Peter was delivered, the saints had a hard time believing Peter had been set free. Warfare Intercession works! Prayer changes things. Expect results when you pray.

Cornelius was another person of prayer. What was so special about Cornelius? He wasn't a Jew. He wasn't even a believer filled with the Holy Ghost. But he was a man who believed in God and was faithful, consistent and diligent in prayer to God and to giving aid to the poor. The prayers and giving of Cornelius created a memorial before the throne of God. And God responded by sending an angel to answer his prayers. This is a third account of God sending an angel in response to prayer.

This account contradicts the theology in John 9:31 that God does not hear the prayers of sinners (based on the formerly blind man's response when being questioned about Jesus). John 9:31...Now we know that God heareth not sinners: but if any man be a worshiper of God, and doeth his will, him he heareth. Cornelius did God's will and was a worshiper. Many Gentile people and sinners within the nation of Israel, made contact with the Lord and their requests were granted. Their faith, diligence in prayer and worship of God got them results. Here are a few:

(1)   Cornelius the Italian, Acts 10:23-48
         He and his family receives Holy Ghost.

(2)   The Centurion, Matthew 8:8, 13
         Servant was healed.

(3)   The Syrophenician Women, Mark 7:26-30
         Daughter was delivered.

(4)   The Thief on the Cross, Luke 23:39-43
         Granted salvation.

(5)   Zacchaeus the Tax Collector, Luke 19:1-10
         Forgiven for stealing.

Acts 10:1...There was a certain man in Caeserea called Cornelius, a centurion of the band called the Italian band, verse 2...A devout man, and one that feared God with all his house, who gave much alms to the people, and prayer to God always. In a vision, the angel instructs Cornelius to send men to Joppa to fetch the Apostle Peter. The angel said Peter will tell you what you ought to do. God had prepared Peter through a trance about clean and unclean foods, that pointed to the salvation of Gentiles through the Gospel of Jesus Christ. Peter went to the house of Cornelius and preached and all that heard his words received the baptism of the Holy Ghost. Acts 10:44-48...These received the Holy Ghost with the initial evidence of speaking in tongues Acts 10:46 and Peter commanded them to be baptized in the name of the Lord. The Lord's name is Jesus Christ; which is consistent with Acts 2:38 and Acts 19:1-6. Because of the prayer life of Cornelius, he and all that were in his house were saved.

The Lord Jesus Christ was the greatest example of prayer. Look at these accounts of how Jesus prayed.

At the tomb of Lazarus, Jesus demonstrated his authority over death by raising a man to life who had been dead for four days. John 11:41-44... Then they took away the stone from the place where the dead was laid. And Jesus lifted up his eyes, and said, Father, I thank thee that thou has heard me. And I knew that thou hearest me always: but because of the people which stand by I said it, that they may believe that thou hast sent me. And when he thus had spoken, he cried with a loud voice, Lazarus, come forth. And he that was dead came forth, bound hand and foot with grave—clothes: and his face was bound about with a napkin. Jesus saith unto them, Loose him, and let him go.

In the 17th chapter of the book of John, Jesus reveals to his disciples and to us all the love that flows from heaven to us. These few words concerning the unity God wants with the followers of Jesus are the love filled words the Great Intercessor prays for us. John 17:20 Neither pray I for these alone, but for them also which shall believe on me through their words:

1 John 2:1-2...My little children, these things write I unto you, that ye sin not. And if any man sin, we have an advocate with the Father, Jesus Christ the righteous: And he is the propitiation for our sins: and not for ours only, but also for the sins of the whole world.

Romans 8:34...Who is he that condemneth? It is Christ that died, yea rather, that is risen again, who is even at the right hand of God, who also maketh intercession for us.

Hebrews 7:24-27 But this man, because he continueth ever, hath an unchangeable priesthood.

Wherefore he is able to also save them to the uttermost that come unto God by him, seeing he ever liveth to make intercession for them. For such an high priest became us, who is holy, harmless, undefiled, separate from sinners, and made higher than the heavens; Who needeth not daily, as those high priests, to offer up sacrifice, first for his own sins, and then for the people's: for this he did once, when he offered up himself.

Because of Jesus we have access to the throne of God through prayer. The Holy Ghost will help us to use this access (Romans 8:26-27) in keeping with the will of God being done in the earth. (...thy will be done on earth as it is in heaven).

Come boldly to God in prayer! Hebrews 4:16... Let us therefore come boldly unto the throne of grace, that we may obtain mercy, and find grace to help in time of need.

I have received testimonies of people who are intercessors. They give accounts of leaving the physical body; going in the spirit to the location of the person in need; and of the person in need seeing the intercessor that was praying for them, come into their presence in a dream or in a vision with their need and/or answer from God. The Spirit is boundless, eternal and infinite. I encourage you to reach out in prayer.

Spiritual Warfare

Chapter 4
The Call to Pray

Luke 18:1...And he spoke a parable unto
them to this end, that men ought
always to pray, and not to faint.

I f you are a parent of a child older than
3 years of age, you have experienced the
impact of relentless requests.

Even if you agree to the child's request, then they
want to know when the request will be granted.
These relentless requests can be unnerving. Such
was the case in the parable of the unjust judge and
the widow.

With our children and with our God, what peace
we have when we can learn to trust that we have
been heard by God, and our request is being
answered by God.

The parable of the Unjust Judge and the Widow is
a great account of continuous, relentless, diligent
and faithful pursuit in prayer.

Luke 18:1...And he spoke a parable unto them to
this end, that men ought always to pray, and not to

faint, Verse 2...Saying, there was in a city a judge, who feared not God, neither regarded man: Verse 3...And there was a widow in that city; and she came unto him, saying, Avenge me of mine adversary. (The adversary is the devil). Verse 4...And he would not for a while: but afterward he said within himself, Though I fear not God, nor regard man, Verse 5...Yet because this widow troubleth me, I will avenge her, lest by her continual coming she weary me. Verse 6...And the Lord said, Hear what the unjust judge saith: Verse 7...And shall not God avenge his own elect, who cry day and night unto him, though he bear long with them? Verse 8...I tell you that he will avenge them speedily. Nevertheless when the Son of man cometh, shall he find faith on the earth?

As an intercessor the Spirit will draft you to pray for someone you don't know, someone on another continent. Many who are sensitive to the Holy Ghost feel the unction to pray at different unscheduled times of the day.

Many are awakened out of their sleep or activities interrupted by the Holy Ghost, unctioning the intercessor to go into immediate action/to go into prayer. Romans 8:26-27...Likewise the Spirit helpeth our infirmities: for we know not what we should pray for as we ought; but the Spirit itself maketh intercession for us with groanings which cannot be uttered. And he that searcheth the hearts knoweth what is the mind of the Spirit, because he maketh intercession for the saints according to the will of God. Another scripture comes to mind: Proverbs 3:5-6...Trust in the Lord with all thine heart, and lean not unto thine own understanding. In all thy ways acknowledge him, and he shall direct thy paths. God will direct our prayers through the Spirit because He knows what is needed.

When I was a teacher at an open bible institute, a student in one of the classes was ill and requested that she be served communion. I told her I would come. Many times we go to do the Lord's work and we do good things and yet miss what it is God wants to do through us. The trip was a little over 25 miles and as I set out, I prayed, "Lord I want to do what you want done." As I prayed, heavy prayer in tongues fell upon me. As I drove, I prayed in tongues until I got to the student's home. I arrived and I set up the communion on the living room coffee table as she and her husband talked. Her mother was standing in the dining room watching and listening. Suddenly the student said, "You know professor, my mama never received the Holy Ghost and she really wants to." I stood and walked towards her mother and I said, "Well you can receive the Holy Ghost now. Do you want to receive the Holy Ghost now?" She said, "Yes," and lifted her hands. I laid hands on her very gently and said, "In the name of Jesus Christ receive the Holy Ghost." She was immediately filled with the Holy Ghost and fell to the floor speaking in tongues. Her daughter yelled, "Don't leave I am going to call one of the neighbors." She was so elated, she had forgotten why I had come. She called a neighbor and the neighbor came right away. She came into the living room. She could see mama still on the floor speaking in tongues. She stared intently. I said, "Lady is there something you want God to do for you?" I asked, "Do want to receive the

Holy Ghost?" She said, "I have always wanted the Holy Ghost." She raised her hands, and she repented of her sins. I gently laid hands on her and she fell to the floor. In a matter of seconds she began to speak in tongues. The student became even more excited and began to call her neighbors. Some were not at home. In a few minutes another lady knocked on the door and came in. Both ladies were still on the floor speaking in tongues. This third lady had a failed kidney condition. I anointed her with oil and prayed the prayer of faith in the name of Jesus Christ for her healing and recovery. Communion was served and prayer was made for the student, also. The Lord really moved in that home that evening. I truly believe that I could have gone and served her communion and that would have been a good thing, yet not the thing the Lord wanted to do. I know that intercession was made in the Spirit and the Lord fulfilled the desires of those ladies to receive the Holy Ghost, because it was God's will. A month later I received a call from the student and she reported her neighbor had been examined and the kidney had began to function. Praise our God who is able and faithful!

Again the scripture says, Romans 8:27...And he that searcheth the hearts knoweth what is the mind of the Spirit, because he maketh intercession for the saints according to the will of God.

Do you know of anyone in a desperate need? Do you know of a serious crisis that only God can solve? Then intercessory prayer is needed. We need to dig in and bombard heaven with prayer. We need to be diligent, persistent, relentless and faithful in our praying. Move the hand of the God, who sent a host of "Flaming Horses and Flaming Chariots" his angels, to protect his prophet Elisha, 2 Kings 6:15-23. The Kingdom of God suffereth violence and the violent taketh it by force. Move the hand of God who commands the Heavenly Host. Move the God of War. This is the will of God being done in the earth.

I will relate these two testimonies in hopes of increasing your faith.

While speaking, a prophet friend of mine remarked that his time for prayer was 12 midnight to 4 a.m. in the morning. He said a certain morning he was praying and a unfamiliar phone number was given to him by the Holy Ghost. He said that he called the number and a lady answered the phone. At the same time, he said the Holy Ghost gave him words and he spoke to the lady, "The Lord says that the child will not die but live, the Lord is delivering the child." He said the woman dropped the phone and began to praise God, he said he could hear her giving praises unto God and dancing. She had a critically ill child in the hospital. The Lord used the Prophet to bring comfort and information that God was working on her behalf.

Don't you want to be a Warfare Intercessor? YES, you do!

Another man I know who prays always and leads prayer services several times a week testified. (I have the date and year recorded in my Day Timer.) He said he was praying on this early Saturday morning and was moved by the Spirit to get up and drive. He said he got into his car and drove, he did not know where he was going, but moved on the unction of the Holy Ghost. He drove and came upon a street and he saw two ladies on the porch of this house. He parked his car and walked to the house. He then greeted the ladies. They began to say you have been sent by God? We were praying that God would send help for our cousin. He went inside and there was a lady in a wheel chair. He began to minister to her. After praying for about twenty minutes, the lady began to spit up black phlegm—gobs of it. God moved and she got up and began to walk. A few days later the lady and a cousin received the Holy Ghost at their home. She came to prayer service and testified. God is moving upon his people and wants to use them in prayer.

Don't you want to be a Warfare Intercessor? Yes, you do!

The scripture reads in Romans 15:4...For whatever things were written aforetime were written for our learning, that we, through patience and comfort of the scriptures, might have hope.

Every person in the scriptures used of God had a great ministry of Intercessory Prayer. We have talked about some of them. In these next pages, we will review examples of commitment to prayer.

There is no better example of a committed prayer life than that of our Lord Jesus Christ.

Mark 1:35...And in the morning, rising up a great while before the day, he went out, and departed into a solitary place, and there prayed. Mark 6:46 And when he had sent them away, he departed into a mountain to pray.

Luke 6:12...And it came to pass in those days, that he went out into a mountain to pray, and continued all night in prayer to God.

Matthew 26:36-46, Mark 14:32-42, Luke 22:39-46, and John 17th Chapter-Describes Jesus agonizing in prayer at Gethsemane. We will use the account in Matthew 26:39-46...And he went a little farther, and fell on his face, and prayed, saying, O my Father, if it be possible, let this cup pass from me; nevertheless, not as I will, but as thou wilt. Verse 40-41... And he cometh unto the disciples, and findeth them asleep; and saith unto Peter; What, could ye not watch with me one hour? Watch and pray, that ye enter not into temptation: the spirit indeed is willing, but the flesh is weak. Verse 41-43...He went away again the second time, and prayed, saying, O my Father, if this cup may not pass away from me, except I drink it, thy will be done. And he came and found them asleep again: for their eyes were heavy.

Verse 44...And he left them, and went away again, and prayed the third time, saying the same words. Luke 22:43-44...And there appeared an angel unto him from heaven, strengthening him. Verse 44... And being in an agony, he prayed more earnestly; and his sweat was as it were great drops of blood falling down to the ground. Jesus prayed fervently and passionately.

In Acts 3:1...Now Peter and John went up together into the temple at the hour of prayer, being the ninth hour. And a certain man, lame from his mother's womb was carried, whom they laid daily at the gate of the temple which is called Beautiful, to ask alms of them that entered into the temple, Who seeing Peter and John about to go into the temple, asked an alms. And Peter, fastening his eyes upon him with John, said Look on us. And he gave heed unto them, expecting to receive something of them. Then Peter said, Silver and gold have I none, but such as I have give I thee: In the name of Jesus Christ of Nazareth rise up and walk. And he took him by the right hand, and lifted him up: and immediately his feet and ankle bones received strength. And he, leaping up stood, and walked, and entered with them into the temple, walking, and leaping, and praising God.

Prayer was a daily part of the Apostles' lives. Their prayer life and study of the scriptures was so important that deacons were appointed to administer the social services of the saints and other business. The Apostles were free to continue their high level of commitment. And it is recorded that two of these deacons had great ministries that were confirmed with mighty signs, wonders and miracles. Acts 6:3-4...Wherefore, brethren, look ye out among you for seven men of honest report, full of the

Holy Ghost and wisdom, whom we may appoint over this business. But we will give ourselves continually to prayer, and to the ministry of the word.

These saints understood the power of prayer, the purpose of prayer and God's will for prayer and His word in their lives and the lives of their leaders.

The Prophetess Anna's testimony is Luke 2:36 And there was one Anna, a prophetess, the daughter of Phanuel, of the tribe of Aser: she was of great age, and had lived with a husband seven years from her virginity; And she was a widow of about fourscore and four years (84 years), who departed not from the temple, but served God with fastings and prayers night and day. And she coming in that instant gave thanks likewise unto the Lord, and spoke of him to all those who looked for redemption in Jerusalem.

Believing Anna could have been married between the ages of 16-21, I believed Anna was between 107-112 years old. What a testimony to serve God with fasting and prayer for such a long time. When rewards are given in heaven many who served the Lord in fasting and prayer will receive great rewards.

Love and concern for others is motivation for prayer ministry.

These saints understood the power of prayer, and the purpose of prayer. The entire church in the earth has to return to prayer now. People would call these Prayer Warriors unbalanced, fanatical, and holier than thou today. They were simply sold out to God.

In class, I tell the students that around the holidays across the nation people line up and get three to five videos and sit down and watch two to ten hours of movies with no problem. If someone in the family decides to give God that kind of attention in prayer, the enemy will get in them and they will become unduly concerned and critical. When you decide that you want to serve God consistently and whole heartedly, you will lose friends and close minister relationships, and your family will become unduly concerned and critical. Does it make sense? No! Yet take the responsibility make the commitment.

Your Commitment: Father, in the precious name of Jesus Christ, help me to pray as I ought. Forgive me for neglecting to pray as I should. At this moment I commit to prayer for your purposes. Lead me in prayer in the Holy Ghost to achieve the things you desire in my life. I make myself available as your vessel of prayer, sensitive to your promptings. AMEN.

Chapter 5

Tongues-
The Language of the Holy Ghost

1 Corinthians 14:2...For he that speaketh in an unknown tongue speaketh not unto men, but unto God; for no man understandeth him; howbeit, in the spirit he speaketh mysteries.

Many great ministers of God around the world have been encouraging saints to pray in the Spirit and/or pray in tongues. Tongues are an infinite medium for prayer because the Spirit is infinite, eternal, ever present, all knowing and all powerful. Many times we pray only in our acquainted language. When we do this, we run out of things to pray for. Our prayers may become repetitious. Praying in tongues is not necessarily the gift of divers tongues, yet it may be. Tongues are not a separate prayer language, but the language of the Holy Ghost. When the Holy Ghost is present in a person so is the language of tongues. Everyone filled with the Holy Ghost can speak in tongues. Speaking in tongues is the first hand evidence (initial evidence), not the only evidence of the infilling of the Holy Ghost. Normally people fight things they have never practiced or they don't

believe in. Praying in tongues is quite scriptural.
1 Corinthians 14:14-15...For if I pray in an unknown tongue, my spirit prayeth, but my understanding is unfruitful. What is it then? I will pray with the spirit, and I will pray with the understanding also: I will sing with the spirit, and I will sing with the understanding also.

Let us examine scripture in support of praying in tongues in faith and love. Unknown Tongues, Divers Tongues, New Tongues, Unrehearsed Tongues, Unlearned Tongues, Interpretation of Tongues, Prophesy, Word of Knowledge and Word of Wisdom are the language of the Holy Ghost. These are how the Holy Ghost speaks. Holy Ghost filled saints will speak in tongues and should have a consistent practice of praying in the Holy Ghost and/or Praying In Tongues. The truth is most people that fight tongues simply do not have the Holy Ghost. 1 Cor. 14 verse 39, Paul cautioned us "forbid not to speak with tongues."

Pray in tongues, pray in the Spirit and you will avail much, and that is bible! James 5:16...The effectual fervent prayer of a righteous man availeth much. We must pray beyond our natural understanding. The church of God is those filled with the Holy Ghost. We must practice the truth.

Let us take a scriptural look at tongues:

In Genesis 11:1...The whole earth was of one language, and of one speech. This is the story of the Tower of Babel. Genesis 11:1-9...The people were of one mind and one effort, but God did not approve of what they were doing and He confounded their language. The building stopped and the people were scattered abroad upon the face of the earth. This is the first account of divers tongues, unlearned and unknown tongues. After some time the tongues did become familiar, common, and developed into languages particular to geographical locations and peoples.

Isaiah 28:11...For with stammering lips and another tongue will he speak to this people. The language of the Holy Ghost is prophesied and is here connected with the refreshing which is Jesus and/or the Holy Ghost. Acts 3:19-20...Repent ye therefore, and be converted, that your sins may be blotted out, when the times of refreshing shall come from the presence of the Lord; and he shall send Jesus Christ, who was before preached unto you.

In Daniel 5:1-31, God writes a message on the wall in the Palace of Belshazzar the king, in the presence of about a thousand people. The king had used the vessels of God for his own lustful revelry. God has some personal things that no one should touch nor use.

The message was written in an unknown language. God could have just as well written the message in a familiar language of anyone there, but He did not. This is not God's way. When Jesus spoke in parables the meanings of the parables were given only to his disciples. Daniel was the servant of God and his prophet, not King Belshazzar.

Amos 3:7...he (God) revealeth his secret unto his servants the prophets.

Instead of speaking in tongues he was writing in tongues which is equivalent. He used his prophet Daniel who was in place to be used of God to demonstrate God's power and knowledge. God used Daniel for his glory by gifting him to give the interpretation of the writing. God knows how to make his people look good because we are clothed with his righteousness.

1 Corinthians 14:2...For he that speaketh in an unknown tongue speaketh not unto men, but unto God: for no man understandeth him; howbeit, in the spirit he speaketh mysteries.

Many intercommunications of the Kingdom are not always for public, demonic dissemination or reception. Communications in tongues are mysteries and/or Top Secret conversations of the Holy Ghost. This is one of the many benefits of speaking in other tongues.

A great man of God used greatly in Deliverance and Spiritual Warfare was speaking one night and encouraged the saints to pray in tongues. He said that the Lord showed him in a dream that demonic forces did not understand prayer in tongues, but that they were familiar with our day to day natural language.

In the natural, wartime high level communications were coded and encrypted, so that enemy forces would not know the movements and strategies of the forces. I believe that the same holds true in the Kingdom of God.

Belshazzar was an evil king who had no regard for God. His kingdom was coming apart and he was coming down from his reign.

This is the writing: Daniel 5:25-28...MENE, MENE, TEKAL, UPHARSIN. God hath numbered thy kingdom, and finished it. Thou art weighed in the balances, and art found wanting. The kingdom is divided, and given to the Medes and Persians.

Again, God could have written the message in a language familiar to someone at the party, but he did not. Romans 11:33-34...O the depth of the riches both of the wisdom and knowledge of God! How unsearchable are his judgments, and his ways past finding out! For who hath known the mind of the Lord? O who hath been his counselor?

God communicates with his people in the Spirit. God speaks to many in part. When God gives prophesies, words of knowledge, and words of wisdom, he is communicating what he wants known in the Spirit to his chosen vessels. When the vessels speak then God's communications are shared.

So God, who separated man's carnal efforts at the Tower of Babel with divers unknown tongues in Genesis 11:1-9; unites his people in the Spirit with the giving of the Holy Ghost, whose presence is identified and evidenced with the speaking of unknown, unlearned divers tongues as the Spirit gave uttterance.

Other occasions of the infilling of the Holy Ghost are in Acts Chapter 10, the house of Corneilius; Acts Chapter 19, Paul ministers to the disciples of John the Baptist, and they received the Baptism of the Holy Ghost and the infilling of the Spirit is initially/immediately evidenced with/by the recipients speaking in tongues.

As we pray in the Spirit we are built up and we are edified according to John 20:21. Paul declares in 1 Corinthians 14:14...For if I pray in an unknown tongue, my spirit prayeth, but my understanding is unfruitful.

Romans 8:26-27...Likewise the Spirit also helpeth our infirmities: for we know not what we should pray for as we ought: but the Spirit maketh intercession for us with groanings which cannot be uttered. And he that searchest the hearts knoweth what is the mind of the Spirit, because he maketh intercession for the saints according to the will of God.

These times of speaking to God from your spirit can fortify you against allowing your soul and body to yield to temptation. Matthew 6:13...And lead us not into temptation, but deliver us from evil: For thine is the kingdom, and the power, and the glory, forever, Amen. We are instructed to ask God to deliver us from evil.

James discusses the evil and the power of the tongue (James chapter 3). Yielding your tongue to the Holy Spirit through praying in tongues results in a saint full of wisdom from Heaven.

Prayer is one of our major spiritual weapons in pulling down the strongholds of the enemy. As we yield to the Holy Ghost, intercession is made through us for the saints and the world in tongues. Romans 8:26-27.

Remembering Answered Prayers

Once our father was hurt badly in a coal mining accident and was hospitalized with a serious back injury. We were out of money and the food was soon exhausted. I remember it was the day before Thanksgiving Day. It was our Mama and seven children; no food and no money. Nothing.

I can remember my mother going into the room and praying. The cook at the school we attended name was Mrs. Shumate. Later that day, there was a knock at the door. It was Mr. Shumate, the cook's husband. He had two big bags of groceries. He said "Maybe you can use this Mrs. Smith." I remember the two big bags of groceries; two chickens and cans of yams and loaves of Jane Parker bread and other goodies. Mama fixed one of the most memorable thanksgiving dinners we ever had.

Mama said that daddy always put offerings in church and that God always was faithful in time of need. I know also that Mama's prayer touched God and God spoke to the Shumates to help us.

Sometimes stop and remember how God answered our prayers.

In conclusion, take the responsibility to pray. Sacrifice idle time for the hour of prayer. Let your day begin and end with prayer and watch what God does in your life everyday. Be consistent in prayer. Prayer is not a special event that comes like a holiday. Prayer is a way of life. Instead of just talking about problems, talk then pray. Instead of gossiping about what people are doing, pray to God to deliver them. Stop complaining about what people are doing to you. Pray, ask God to bless them.

Launch out into the deep. Prayer should be every saints ministry. Do not just leave all the praying to those you regard as prayer warriors and church intercessors. Gain some prayer experiences of your own. Jesus prayed, ministered to people as God directed and returned to communion with the Father through prayer.

As God directs, keep a Prayer Journal to remind you of what you prayed for and how and when God answered your request. As you learn about the power of prayer, share it with your family and friends. God's Kingdom will be glorified through the fruit of answered prayer.

Vocabulary

(1) Agreement - the coming together, uniting or united agreement about the things of God.

(2) Bind - to tie up, restrain thus frustrating ability and/or freedom. Matthew 18:18...Verily I say unto you, Whatsoever ye shall bind on earth shall be bound in heaven: Speaking in the name of Jesus Christ and binding demonic activities on earth will bind the activities in heaven.

(3) Faith - Hebrew 11:1...Now Faith is the substance of things hoped for, and the evidence of things not seen.

(4) Hope – the constant anticipation of receiving good from God.

(5) Intercession – the act of prayer and/or pleading on behalf of another. Vines states it this way: A technical term for approaching a King.

(6) Loose – release, take away restraint and/or set free. Matthew 18:18...And whatsoever ye shall loose on earth shall be loosed in heaven. Jesus speaks to a woman with a spirit of infirmity. Luke 13:12... Woman, thou art loosed from thine infirmity. Verse 13...she was made straight.

(7) Persistent – (as it relates to prayer) is the diligent, fervent, relentless initiative of prayer.

(8) Posture – standing, kneeling or prostrate are some positions we employ when we pray.

(9) Prayer – a request made unto God Almighty.

(10) Prayer in the Spirit – praying in the Holy Ghost/praying in tongues.

(11) Repetitious Prayers – learned and practiced prayers.

(12) Unknown Tongue – the unrehearsed, unlearned language of the Holy Ghost.

Spiritual Warfare

Warfare
Worshiper
Part 2

Your Worship is
in spirit and truth
and aimed towards
the throne of God. It
transcends your earthly
location and beckons the
glory, power, and presence
of God to our circumstances.
It breaks yokes, looses bands,
and lifts heavy burdens, freeing
the spirit, soul, and body for
renewing, healing, transformation,
and growth. Your worship is
personally therapeutic and
delivers those in your immediate
presence and all that hear it.

Shiral, my lovely wife of 30 years,

I salute you for over 30 years

you have labored in

Praise and Worship.

May God's Anointing and Favor

take you higher in His Presence.

Chapter 1
Warfare Worshiper

1 Samuel 16:23...And it came to pass, when
the evil spirit from God was upon Saul,
that David took an harp, and played with
his hand, so Saul was refreshed, and was
well, and the evil spirit departed from him.

In the Old Testament and New Testament
another way warfare is conducted and
accomplished is through praise and worship.

Praise (Judah)-is the deliberate choice to use our
physical instruments to give glory to God, and/or
commend God through dancing, the playing of
instruments, the singing of songs and with the
speaking of our voices, testimonies of God's good-
ness and combinations of the aforementioned.

In Psalms 150, we who have breath are constrained
to Praise God.

Worship-is the deliberate addressing and touching
of God in the spirit. It is communion with God in the
Spirit. In worship, we give reverence, honor, glory,

and adoration to the Lord, with our spirit in the Holy Ghost. Worship is about who God is.

Jesus revealed to us in John 4:24…and they that worship him must worship him in spirit and in truth. This level of communion can only be accomplished through the Holy Ghost. Only in the Spirit are we one with God.

1. Our first account of Warfare Worship is that of David. 1 Samuel 16:14…But the Spirit of the Lord departed from Saul, and an evil spirit from the Lord troubled him. In verse 15 and 16 it is recorded that Saul's servants understood his condition and they requested that if they could send for a skilled musician to play, Saul would be well.

1 Samuel 16:23…And it came to pass, when the evil spirit from God was upon Saul, that David took a harp, and played with his hand: so Saul was refreshed, and was well, and the evil spirit departed from him.

David had a relationship with God and played before God and to God daily. David praised God for using him to slay the lion and the bear. So David, the anointed harpist, played skillfully and touched God, and God's presence overshadows David's surrounding and Saul was made well.

Musicians, music must be holy, in spirit and in truth,

pleasing unto God. His anointing will set the captive free. Purpose your music for God.

One thing that many in the Bible seemed to have on many of us today is the recognition of demon spirits. The servants of Saul knew that his condition was caused by an evil spirit. A spirit that caused an indifferent attitude, a condition of heaviness came upon Saul. This spirit is described in Isaiah 61:3...To appoint unto them that mourn in Zion, to give unto them beauty for ashes, the oil of joy for mourning, the garment of praise for the spirit of heaviness.

Today many Christians and others have evil spirits, evil conditions that can be healed by worship. They can participate in worship with others or be ministered to by an anointed singer/musician/choir in a similar fashion as Saul was.

In this particular account there was discerning of the spirit by the servants, there was also intercession (the seeking of help) by the servants, and the Warfare Worship conducted by David, God's anointed. This lesson teaches us that our temple musicians and singers must reach for the mark of the high calling in worship. It goes unnoticed but in temple service after temple service many are set free and healed through the ministry of anointed music.

Believe me, I know everyone does not have a pleasant singing voice nor can everyone sing skillfully, but I believe that all ministers must serve God in Praise and Worship. God requires praise and worship, he demands it. Sometimes the purposes of God are not always afforded the convenience of anointed musicians and singers, neither is it always expedient or affordable. Remember, we are perfecting.

So the minister must have a personal life of worship and carry the anointing as one submitted to God in worship. God's minister should praise and worship always. Pastors and leaders of ministries must be praisers and worshipers, individually and corporately. We must lead in praise and worship, constrain others to worship and must be observed praising and worshiping our God. Praise and worship is a warfare life style. We must praise, we must worship God.

2. Our second account of Warfare Worship is in Joshua 6:1-27. The Lord instructed Joshua that he had given Jericho into Joshua's hands and he gave Joshua specific instructions on how to carry out the Warfare Campaign. We must have a Word from God and obey the Word to have good success.

Joshua received specific instructions from God's Word. This was directed by Joshua. First in verse 3...Ye shall compass the city, all ye men of

Spiritual Warfare

war, and go round about the city once. Thus shalt thou do six days. Calling for the men of war was a sign of eminent confrontation. Ephesians 6:11...Put on the whole armor of God...next, the seven priests shall bear before the ark seven trumpets of rams horns. The priest are God's anointed and appointed bearing the presence of God. Further instructing, the seventh day ye shall compass the city seven times, and the priest shall blow with the trumpets. The 7th day, the 7 trumpets, the seven priests represents the completeness of obedience and the finish of the confrontation. And the result, it shall come to pass that, when they make a long blast with the rams horn, and when ye hear the sound of the trumpet. The sound of the trumpets was the announcing the coming of the Lord and the prompting of the people to praise Him; all the people shall shout with a great shout; and the wall of the city shall fall down flat, and the people went up into the city, every man straight before him, and they took the city. And they utterly destroyed their enemy. Don't wait until the Battle is over, Shout Now! Obedience to praise and worship of our God brings victory.

3. Our third account is found in Mark 10:46. ...Blind Bartimaeus shouted to the Lord to help him. Bartimaeus cried loudly, thou Son of David have mercy on me! In his cry he declared Jesus to

be of royal heritage, a king and he declared Jesus had the power to heal him. This is Worship. Jesus heard his praise and healed him. Many Psalms begin with a verse that constrains us and gives us instructions to worship the Lord our God. When every Holy Ghost filled child of God begins to live these instructions, church services will be electric and the King of Glory shall come in. We must come to his temple to touch him with our praise and worship. Knowing that we are creating an environment for healing, deliverance, and salvation.

Psalms 100:4...Enter into his gates with thanks-giving, and into his courts with praise: be thankful unto him, and bless his name.

Psalms 103:1...Bless the Lord, O my soul, and all that is within me, bless his holy name. How shall I bless Him? ...with all that is within me.

Psalms 145:1...I will extol thee, my God, O King, and I will bless thy name forever and ever. Extol means to praise with great enthusiasm, pleasure and with high regard and wonder.

Psalms 147:1...Praise ye the Lord: for it is good to sing praises unto our God; for it is pleasant: and praise is comely (fitting).

In Matthew 6:9...Jesus is instructing the disciples how to pray: He says to address the Father and hallow his name. After this manner, therefore, pray ye: Our Father which art in heaven, Hallowed be thy name.

Hallow means to make holy, respect, revere and/or set apart for God. We are to begin our prayers with thanksgiving, praise and worship. Remember we are approaching the throne of the King of Kings, the Lord of Lords, God Almighty. He is worthy of all of our praise. Come boldly and come correct.

Deuteronomy 6:5...And thou shalt love the Lord thy God with all thine heart, and with all thy soul, and with all thy might. Look at the required level of service toward God. With our ALL. Worship of this caliber is a mighty weapon against the forces of darkness.

4. Our fourth account of Warfare Worship is found in the book of Acts 16:16-35...Paul and Silas were jailed after casting out a spirit of divination out of a woman. Her deliverance spelled economic disaster for her masters. She was a psychic, soothsayer, and fortune teller. Casting out the spirit was one phase of warfare that set the woman free. The retaliation caused Paul and Silas to be put in prison.

We will look at the severity of their state. There is no record of any complaint of their beaten condition, of their pain and injury nor a request for God to deliver them. Acts 16:22-24...The magistrates rent off their clothes, and commanded to beat them. And when they had laid many stripes upon them, they cast them into prison, charging the jailer to keep them safely: Who, having received such a charge, thrust them into the inner prison, and made their feet fast in the stocks. Paul and Silas were cast into a prison inside the prison or the maximum security prison and had their feet bound in stocks. Put in prison for serving the Lord! Again, there is no record of them complaining of their beaten condition, of their pain, nor a request for God to deliver them.

Acts 16:25-26...And at midnight Paul and Silas prayed, and sang praises unto God; and the prisoners heard them. (God heard them.) And suddenly there was a great earthquake, so that the foundation of the prison were shaken; and imme-diately all the doors were opened, and everyone's bands were loosed.

Understand that their prayer, praise, and worship touched God in their bondage. God shook the foundation of what was holding them—the prison. Every level of bondage released them. All the doors were opened and everyone's bands were loosed. This means that the people around them bands were loosed. Four levels of spiritual bondage. These people did not praise God, but heard Paul and Silas praying and praising. Such was the move of God that the jailer asked, "What must I do to be saved?" Then Paul set the jailer and his family free through the Gospel of Jesus Christ. After God's work was done, Paul and Silas' wounds were dressed. Finally ultimate freedom, Acts 16:35... And when it was day, the magistrates sent the sergeants, saying, Let those men go.

Worship leader, your worship will set you free on every level. Your worship will set those who hear you free. And such will be the move of God that someone will say, "What must I do to be saved?"

Worship Brings Deliverance and Healing

5. Our fifth account in Warfare Worship is found in Mark 5, the demoniac at Gadara. This incident is remarkable in that the demoniac was set free from every spirit. He was healed and his mind was restored.

Mark 5:1...And they came over unto the other side of the sea, into the country of the Gadarenes.

Verse 2...And when he was come out of the ship, immediately there met him out of the tombs a man with an unclean spirit,

Verse 3...Who had his dwelling among the tombs; and no man could bind him, no, not with chains:

Verse 4...He had been often bound with fetters and chains, and the chains had been plucked asunder by him, and the fetters broken in pieces; neither could any man tame him.

Verse 5...And always, night and day, he was in the mountains, and in the tombs, crying, and cutting himself with stones.

Verse 6...But when he saw Jesus afar off, he ran and worshiped him.

Verse 7...And cried with a loud voice, and said, What have I to do with thee, Jesus, thou Son of the Most High God? I adjure thee by God, that thou torment me not.

I pose a question here. Was it the possessed man who ran and worshiped the Lord or was it a fearful demon who guided the possessed man to run to worship and inquire about his fate?

In the scripture, it is all the possessed man could do to run to worship the only one that could help him. The demon worshiped begging to know his fate. Notice in verse 7 that the demon prays to the Most High God that Jesus not torment him. Jesus permits the demons to go into the swine and the man is set free.

Spiritual Warfare

Verse 8...For he said unto him, Come out of the man, thou unclean spirit.

Verse 15...And they come to Jesus, and see him that was possessed with the devil, and had the legion, sitting, and clothed, and in his right mind;

6. The sixth account of Warfare Worship is that of the Syrophenician Woman-Matthew 15:21-28.

Matthew 15:21-28...Then Jesus went (from there) and departed into the coasts of Tyre and Sidon. And behold, a woman of Canaan came out of the same coasts, and cried unto him, saying, Have mercy on me, O Lord, thou Son of David; my daughter is grievously vexed with a devil. But he answered her not a word. And his disciples came and besought him, saying, Send her away; for she crieth after us. But he answered and said, I am not sent but unto the lost sheep of the house of Israel. Then she came and worshiped him, saying, Lord, help me. But he answered and said, It is not meet to take the children's bread, and to cast it to dogs. And she said, Truth Lord: yet the dogs eat of the crumbs which fall from their master's table. Then Jesus answered and said unto her, O woman great is thy faith: be it unto thee even as thou wilt. And her daughter was made whole from that very hour.

This mother had faith that Jesus could help her. She would not leave until she got the Lord's help.

She worshiped the Lord. She swallowed any pride that she might have had, because the Lord called her and her daughter dogs.

The scripture declares in Matthew 7:7, 8...Ask, and it shall be given you; seek, and ye shall find; knock, and it shall be opened unto you: For every one that asketh receiveth; and he that seeketh findeth; and to him that knocketh it shall be opened.

This mother came for help for her demonized daughter. She was relentless, diligent and persistent. After being initially turned away by Jesus, she worshiped the Lord. Her worship got the Lord's attention, he acknowledged her faith and her daughter was healed. Amen.

7. The seventh account of Warfare Worship is the Leper in Matthew 8:1-3.

Matthew 8:1-3...When he was come down from the mountain, great multitudes followed him. And, behold, there came a leper and worshiped him, saying, Lord, if thou wilt, thou canst make me clean. And Jesus put forth his hand, and touched him saying, I will, be thou clean. And immediately his leprosy was cleansed.

The leper knew the Lord's power and ability to help him. He declares if Jesus wanted to or desired to he could heal him. Jesus says, Yes, I will. It is not recorded that he cried unclean as the law demanded, because he was a leper. He came to Jesus just as he was. Don't let your condition or position stop you from coming to the Lord for help. Come boldly! The Lord is Faithful.

Many times people desire help from God. But many times they ask incorrectly and approach the Lord inappropriately. In approaching the Lord, we should pray as he told us.

He told us to ask the Father in the name of Jesus Christ. We are to hallow his name, worship that name, worship him and then let our request be known unto God.

Worship is for God only. Worship pleases him. When we approach God for anything, let us always remember that we are going before the Heavenly throne of the King of Kings. We are to worship and give him honor, for he is worthy of all our praise and worship.

WARFARE IN GIVING–I suppose we never thought of waging spiritual warfare through our giving, yet Warfare Giving is a biblical principal and should be part of our worship. Our study takes us to Malachi the 3rd chapter. Read the whole chapter at your first opportunity.

Malachi 3:3...that they may offer unto the Lord

an offering in righteousness. Verse 4...Then shall the offering of Judah and Jerusalem be pleasant unto the Lord, as in the days of old, and as in the former years.

Malachi 3:7...Even from the days of your fathers ye are gone away from mine ordinances, and have not kept them. Return unto me, and I will return unto you, saith the Lord of hosts. But ye said, Wherein shall we return? Look how the Lord is described, The Lord of Hosts or The Lord of His Army. Malachi 3:8...Will a man rob God? Yet ye have robbed me. But ye say, Where in have we robbed thee? In tithes and offerings.

TITHE-is a tenth of income or prosperity. The giving of or returning of the tenth to God, for God's work. The tithe can be thought of in this manner. To earn money we exchange talent, service, time, effort, and strength for a certain wage or salary. We are giving or returning to God a tenth of our talent, service, time, effort, sweat, worry and strength expended to gain the wage, salary, money, or exchanged good. Money represents life and service. Give the tenth to God of our life/living that our nine tenths may be blessed.

OFFERING-to bring a gift, an offer, a libation, a contribution, a financial (or thing of value) contribution, something presented for acceptance.

An offering can be a giving beyond or below the tithe. Not as much as a tithe or offering beyond the tithe. I give my tithes plus an offering.

Malachi 3:10...Bring ye all the tithes into the storehouse, that there may be meat in mine house, and try me now herewith, saith the Lord of Host, if I will not open for the windows of heaven, and pour you out a blessing, that there shall not be room enough to receive it.

Malachi 3:11...And I will rebuke the devourer for your sakes, and he shall not destroy the fruits of your ground, neither shall your vine cast her fruit before the time in the field, saith the Lord of Hosts.

These scriptures bear repeating. The Lord of Host (His Army) will rebuke the devourer (the devil), (whose purpose is John 10:10...to steal, kill, and destroy); the Lord rebukes the devourer for our sakes, for our benefit, for our well being.

And this rebuke results in stopping the enemy's ability to destroy what God has blessed us with.

God will abundantly bless us in our warfare through giving, and rebuke the devourer for our sakes.

Spiritual Warfare

Mark 16:17
... In my name shall they cast out devils

Warfare
Casting Out Devils
Part 3

You, by Faith,
in the Name of
Jesus Christ, shall
expel devils from the
personage, habitat and
affairs of the afflicted.
By the authority of God in
the name of Jesus Christ,
you release the captive, free
the demonized, forge an immediate
assault against the kingdom of
darkness. The time is urgent! The
battle is raging! You will confront
and defeat principalities and
powers!

Dedication

To Bishop, Dr. Ralph E. Green.

Thank you for the 30 years with you
in ministry. The observation of the
Demonstration of the Power of the
Holy Ghost is a precious lesson for me in
ministry. You are a Great Man of God.
I see you live the scriptures.

Chapter 1
A Workman That Needeth Not Be Ashamed

2 Timothy 2:15...Study to show thyself approved
unto God, a workman that needeth not be
ashamed, rightly dividing the word of truth.

There Is Some Shameful Stuff Going Forth
In Ministry! It Should Not Be! The following
is not an accusation, but what some ministers actually do. If the shoe fits, wear it. For the innocent
and the victimized I apologize on behalf of Our
Lord and those who minister with integrity.

Casting out Devils and Spiritual Warfare is not for
the unlearned or the immature novice. This is the
Lord's Work and Ministry. This is serious work.
The disciples were taught by the Master about
three and one half years with on the job training
and observation of Jesus ministering. After the
Lord's resurrection he gave them an additional
forty day Post Graduate course.

The scripture declares in 2 Timothy 2:15...Study to
show thyself approved unto God, a workman that

needeth not be ashamed rightly dividing the word of truth. Rightly dividing the word means to have understanding and act accordingly. It means to act according to how the word is written and should be executed.

Sometimes ministering calls for restraint and you have to truly know what you are doing. There are horrible stories where people have been choked to death by someone who simply did not know what they were doing. Recently, a young boy died from what has been called an exorcism and he may have been smothered to death. Others have been physically beaten supposedly driving the evil spirit out and the person was beaten to death. These recent events have gotten world media attention. This brings distrust and doubt to many ministries.

Ministry has to be done in the Holy Ghost by the leading of the Spirit, and not out of presumption, imitation, affectation or in craftiness.

Ephesians 6:12...For we wrestle not against flesh and blood...

Again, casting out devils and spiritual warfare is not for the unlearned, immature novice. This is the Lord's Work and Ministry. This ministry is serious work.

I was a Washington, D.C. police officer for ten
years. I have seen angry people, mental patients
and the drug user hurt themselves because of them
resisting and/or fighting from demonic influence,
emotional adrenaline and or drug induced ability.
I have heard bones crack and seen people receive
injury from the struggle. Truthfully, some injuries of
both parties would have been avoided if situations
were handled quickly, knowledgeably and without
fear. In some instances there was no way to avoid
injury.

I remember being called to a supermarket where
the manager saw a large woman stuffing meat into
a big purse. Another officer and I approached her
cautiously. We took the purse from her and the
manager and I examined it. It was stuffed with
assorted meats. We were standing about six feet
from her and the other officer was standing slightly
behind her. She said, "You got the meat back, can
I go?" At that point the other officer said you are
going to jail and slapped one handcuff on one of
her wrist. This lady was very tall and very strong.
She immediately began to resist and threw the
other officer into the meat counter. His reflex
action was to lift the cuffed hand behind her in-
ducing pain until she surrendered, but again she
was strong and resisted even more. I immediately
came and assisted. The lady was resisting with such

great force that I heard her joints and bones crack-ing. I screamed at her, "Lady, Stop it! Stop it! Before you get hurt." Thank God she did stop immediately. She surrendered and began to cry. I was relieved. She did not deserve a broken arm or wrist for some stolen meat. What does this have to do with casting out demons? People are not to be beat up or killed by the minister, because they need deliverance. God help us all!

I have come into contact with people who had demons in them. When initial prayer was made, not much happened. The spirits had been around for years. Jesus said these kind come only by fasting and prayer. I walked away and came back after touching God on their behalf in prayer.

The scripture says, "We wrestle not against flesh and blood." There has to be a loosening in the Spirit. Some ministers feel like they are under the gun to perform. No, we are called to obey God and minister in the Holy Ghost.

Once a minister and I were called to a home where a young girl had driven her fist through the walls. Her hands were swollen and she was talking out of her head. She was slim and weighed about 100 pounds. We prayed and nothing happened. The Spirit guided me to talk to her. Suddenly, she began speaking in a young child's voice and she also began to cry. Her sister related that they were taken from their mother at a young age and she began to cry, also. I could tell that the problem was a family matter and generational in nature. We prayed again and nothing happened. We retreated and told the family and friends to bring her to the evening service without fail. They agreed to bring her. We left to intercede on their behalf. I could have stayed and ministered out of my own desire to see her set free. I could have tired her out in the flesh, but thank God I didn't.

Deliverance is a supernatural act of the Holy Ghost. It is not by man's will or might, but by the power of the Holy Ghost. I remembered someone commenting as I entered the sanctuary that evening; they said, you look like you're mad at somebody. I said "I've been in warfare. I'm mad at the devil."

I alerted the speaker that a young lady was coming for deliverance. I told him what had taken place that morning, and that I had been in prayer for her. I told him I would be sitting in the pews. He preached a short message and made the altar call. He called for the young lady. She came down with her sister. The elder motioned for me to come. I came and led the young lady into repentance and forgiveness. The Holy Ghost had shown me spirits of fear, anger, loneliness, generational attachments, and unforgiveness. I said to her, "This will be hard but call the names of the people that hurt you, and say Lord I choose to forgive them." When she did this, the power of God fell upon her and her sister and they fell to the floor. The spirits came out and they were set free in a few minutes in the name of Jesus. She and her sister walked out of church that night smiling and rejoicing, being set free by the power of God.

When demons are cast out, many times people fall to the floor or are thrown to the floor. Sometimes spirits speak out, and other times the spirits scream as they make their exit. Sometimes people vomit or throw up phlegm and/or convulse. This is the description of casting out demons throughout the scriptures. We can't redefine it. We can't rescind the scriptures and develop our own modus operandi (method of operation). Let us operate by the scriptures.

Ministers need to minister in integrity. Trying to make yourself look good and look powerful usually leads to a fall and makes honest ministers look bad. This is not a show. Casting out devils is God's work and the mission and/or commission of the church. Mark 16:17, Matthew 10:7-8.

I am personally tired of ministers pushing people down, slapping people in the head and literally knocking people in the floor. This is just a

counterfeit of the power of God. What a shame
and a sham. I have spoken with young people
after such demonstrations. Young people are very
honest. They testified they had been slapped in
the head and knocked to the floor. Some said
that to stop the pushing, they just fell to the floor.
Ministers need not slap, push or attempt to give the
appearance of some power of God. God does not
need that kind of help. He wants us to be honest
in our ministering.

In service one night, I went to the altar for prayer.
I observed a minister going from person to person.
He was hitting them. I said, "Lord if that preacher
hits me, there is going to be trouble." I prayed,
"Lord when he stands in front of me you touch me
before he gets a chance." I tell you that the Lord
knew I was not playing, and he was faithful. As the
minister approached me a wonderful overpowering
touch from God laid me in the floor. When I did get
up, every step was like stepping in puddles of glory!

Ministers, our work in the name of Jesus has eternal
consequences. Don't let your works be of the
flesh, because they will be of wood and stubble
and unable to stand the fire of God's judgement.
Integrity in ministry is vital.

Spiritual Warfare

Chapter 2
Know Your Adversary

2 Corinthians 2:10-11...To whom ye forgive
any thing, I forgive also: for if I forgave
any thing, to whom I forgave it, for your
sakes forgave I it in the person of Christ.
Lest Satan should get an advantage of us;
for we are not ignorant of his devices.

God is sovereign, infinite, eternal, all powerful, all knowing and is ever present. God
stretched forth the heavens alone. Our God is the
ultimate power.

It is War Time and the church should know the adversary. During every war waged by America, there
was the gathering of intelligence. The gathering
of intelligence was information about the enemy
forces. We knew who the enemy was, where the
enemy was, where and who the enemy was attack-
ing and his modus operandi, (the enemy's method
of operation).

2 Corinthians 2:10-11...To whom ye forgive any thing,
I forgive also: for if I forgave any thing, to whom I
forgave it, for your sakes forgave I it in the person

of Christ. Lest Satan should get an advantage of us; for we are not ignorant of his devices.

Paul says here, don't regret, forgiveness is necessary , Lest Satan should get the advantage of us...for we are not ignorant of his devices. We are not ignorant of his strategies, conspiracies and his plans to steal, kill and destroy.

When the devil tempted the Lord Jesus in the wilderness, it is clear that the devil had knowledge of the Word of God and knew the Word of God. The devil has had about 6,000 years to study man. The enemy studies us and watches for a chance to enter in. We can not afford to be careless and self-willed in this warfare. We must study the Word of God to understand how the devil works.

In a natural war, the soldier has to thoroughly familiarize himself/herself with their particular weapon of choice or assignment. The soldier must keep the weapon clean, lubricated, and maintain it in perfect working order for immediate use. Saints must adapt this same mind set.

We must use our weapons of warfare and armor of warfare to defeat the enemy.

Satan knows the importance of the truth that the Word of God presents to the human heart.

In Mark chapter 4, Jesus teaches us about the devices Satan effectively uses to steal God's Word from our heart. Know these devices! Stop the devil from stealing from you.

Casting out Devils is a part of ministry that many more people in the Body of Christ must begin to practice. As said in the previous chapter, Casting out Devils is not a specialized ministry relegated only to the Deliverance minister. The scripture declares it is...to them that believe. Mark 16:17

What is casting out demons or devils? It means that In the name of Jesus Christ, a minister expels or drives away a spirit or spirits from a person. This action breaks the yoke, or loosens the band or grip of the enemy. The action may also lift heavy burdens, and drive away infirmities of sickness from the person's temple. This action brings about healing, wholeness, and freedom to that individual.

Isaiah 10:27...and the yoke shall be destroyed because of the anointing. Such as spirits of infirmity, Luke 13:11, spirits of heaviness, Isaiah 61:3 and spirits of fear, 2 Timothy 1:7.

Again how were demons cast out and defeated in the Scriptures.

Speaking the Word of God
Luke 4:1-13...Jesus withstood Satan by speaking
the Word of God.

In the Name of Jesus
Mark 16:17...And these signs shall follow them that
believe; In my name shall they cast out devils.
Luke 10:17...And the seventy returned again with
joy, saying, Lord, even the devils are subject unto
us through thy name. Acts 16:18...But Paul, being
grieved, turned and said to the spirit, I command
thee, in the name of Jesus Christ, to come out of
her. And he came out the same hour.

Working of Miracles
Acts 19:11-12...And God wrought special miracles
by the hands of Paul: So that from his body were
brought unto the sick handkerchiefs or aprons,
and the diseases departed from them, and evil
spirits went out of them.

Laying on of Hands
Luke 13:12-13...And when Jesus saw her, he called
her to him, and said unto her, Woman thou art
loosed from thine infirmity. And he laid his hands
on her: and immediately she was made straight,
and glorified God.

Let us examine Through the laying on of hands.
People say that Jesus never layed hands on people
to cast out devils, yet in the scriptures he did.

Luke 13:13...And he laid his hands on her; and immediately she was made straight, and glorified God. The spirit of infirmity left and the woman was healed.

I would like to interject some testimonies. When initially ministering, demonic activity was not obvious nor discerned. As I laid hands on individuals demons spoke, cursed, fought and/or declared their purpose for being there.

One example, a lady came forward and said that she had labored breathing and severe pain in her chest. She had consulted the doctor who could not give a diagnosis of the symptoms. I told her it could be a spirit. When we laid hands on her and began to rebuke the condition. A demon of murder spoke out of her, and said, "Leave her alone, just leave her alone, she is supposed to die." He repeated the words, "Leave her alone. She is supposed to die." I had placed the microphone to her mouth and many in the audience heard in amazement. God is faithful. We cast the demon out in the name of Jesus Christ.

On another occasion, a lady came forward and said she had not been able to swallow for about three months. She had consulted a doctor and the doctor could not give a diagnosis for the condition. I told her it was a spirit. As we laid hands on her, the spirit began to scream. The woman gagged and spit up phlegm. After the spirit had left, she ate food in front of the audience in that service and praised God.

In this same service, I laid hands on a lady, deaf in both ears and prayed. The deaf spirits left her and she could hear again 100 percent. She testified that she could not hear the message I gave on that morning. The Lord healed her perfectly.

On numerous occasions, on purpose or indirectly, by shaking hands and/or touching people; demons began to curse me and suddenly flee my presence. Other spirits cried out "No, No leave us alone, you can't have him," but were cast out by the power of God in the name of Jesus Christ.

A great preacher, a well known soul winner was ministering one night and my pastor was standing with him ministering, when a demon began to speak out of a person receiving prayer. The preacher jumped behind my pastor and peered inquisitively from around the side of him. My pastor cast the spirit out of the person. The minister said that he did not mess with demons. Wow! Did you hear what you just read?

There are some things unfamiliar to us that may startle us. Remember we are learning new things every day.

On another occasion, another well known preacher preached a mighty message and as a great prayer line formed, he told the people to return to their seats. He took an offering. Our pastor prayed for the people. When asked why he did not pray for the people, he said, preaching was his gift. He did not pray for anyone. Wow! Did you hear what I just said?

We can come to the conclusion that ministers don't cast out devils because:

1. They may need the devil cast out of them.

2. They are ignorant of the scriptures, and what their responsibility is.

3. They are afraid and fearful.

4. They don't know how and have never done it, and don't want to do it.

5. They don't believe in Casting Out Devils.

6. They are lazy. Many say casting out devils drains their strength.

7. They are ill prepared to cast out devils.

8. They have never had to or never had the opportunity to.

9. They tried and failed.

10. Some say that casting out demons requires a special anointing.

11. Some say it is not their cup of tea. They are just disobedient.

12. Truthfully, some have been prevented by leadership.

13. Many don't love the people enough to want to see them walk in complete freedom.

Mark 16:17...Jesus says these signs will follow them that believe, in my name shall they cast out devils. Jesus charged us to preach the gospel to every creature, heal the sick, cleanse the leper, raise the dead and cast out devils.

The Gospel of Mark records 18 references to Spiritual Warfare/casting out devils. (Some may count differently.)

(1) Mark 1:12-13   Jesus is tempted by Satan in the wilderness 40 forty days.

(2) Mark 1:23-26   Jesus cast out devils at the synagogue.

(3) Mark 1:30-31   Fever in Peter's mother rebuked.

(4) Mark 1:32-33   They brought those possessed with devils.

(5) Mark 1:34	Jesus cast out many demons.	
(6) Mark 1:39	Jesus cast out demons in other places	
(6) Mark 3:11	Demons recognize Jesus/ Jesus cast out demons.	
(7) Mark 3:14, 15	The Disciples chosen/authority given to cast out demons.	
(8) Mark 3:22-30	Accusation made against Jesus casting out demons.	
(9) Mark 5:2-13	Demons cast out of the man at the tombs/Gadara.	
(10) Mark 6 :7	The twelve sent forth to preach the kingdom, cast devils...	
(11) Mark 6:13	The twelve cast out devils	
(12) Mark 7:25-30	The Syrophenician woman's daughter delivered from a demon.	
(13) Mark 9:14-18	Disciples fail to cast spirit out of boy.	
(14) Mark 9:19-28	Jesus cast the deaf and dumb spirit out of the boy.	
(15) Mark 9:29	Jesus references some demons come forth by prayer & fasting	

(16) Mark 9:38-39 Someone outside of the twelve
                    is found casting out demons.

(17) Mark 16:9   Reference to Mary Magdalene
                    being delivered from 7 demons.

(18) Mark 16:17   The prophetic word: In my
                    name shall they cast out
                    demons...

Some of these accounts are also recorded in the
other Gospels.

In Isaiah, we read of the responsibility of knowing
God's word.

Isaiah 28:9...Whom shall he teach knowledge? And
whom shall he make to understand doctrine? Them
who are weaned from the milk, and drawn from the
breasts. The mature must hear, obey and practice
the word of God.

Scriptural References:
Isaiah 28:10...For precept must be upon precept,
precept upon precept: line upon line, line upon line;
here a little, and there a little. The scriptures build
a strong case of evidence for active warfare and
casting out devils. There is evidence in the book
of Isaiah 14:12-17, Ezekiel 28:11-19, Job the 1st and
2nd chapter, Daniel 10:10-21, The Gospels, Acts 8:7,
Acts 16:16-18, and Acts 19:11-20.

Chapter 3
The Origin of Satan

Ezekiel 28:12-15...Thou sealest up the sum, full of wisdom, and perfect in beauty. Thou hast been in Eden the garden of God; every precious stone was thou covering, the sardius, topaz, and the diamond, the beryl, the onyx, and the jasper, the sapphire, the emerald, and the carbuncle, and gold; the workmanship of thy tabrets and of thy pipes was prepared in thee in the day thou was created. Thou art the anointed cherub that covereth, and I have set thee so: thou wast upon the holy mountain of God; thou has walked up and down in the midst of the stones of fire. Thou was perfect in thy ways from the day that thou was created.

Some may ask, So where did demons come from? Who is this Satan, the Devil, and Lucifer? Lucifer was the anointed cherubim. An angel of high order, of great beauty and extra-ordinary gifts, talents and abilities. Lucifer from his beginning was a angelic being who was music to the Lord. An angelic being like no other with built-in instrumentation, whose design reflected the glory of God. Look at the description of Lucifer given in scripture.

Ezekiel 28:12-15...Thou sealest up the sum, full of wisdom, and perfect in beauty. Thou hast been in Eden the garden of God; every precious stone was thou covering, the sardius, topaz, and the diamond, the beryl, the onyx, and the jasper, the sapphire, the emerald, and the carbuncle, and gold; the workmanship of thy tabrets and of thy pipes was prepared in thee in the day thou was created. Thou art the anointed cherub that covereth, and I have set thee so: thou wast upon the holy mountain of God; thou has walked up and down in the midst of the stones of fire. Thou was perfect in thy ways from the day that thou was created. I am sure many ask, Lucifer had all this, what happened?

Ezekiel 28:15-17...till iniquity was found in thee. By the multitude of thy merchandise they have filled the midst of thee with violence, and thou hast sinned: therefore, I will cast thee as profane out of the mountain of God, and I will destroy thee, O covering cherub, from the midst of the stones of fire. Thine heart was lifted up because of thy beauty, thou has corrupted thy wisdom by reason of thy brightness: I will cast thee to the ground, I will lay thee before kings, that they may behold thee.

Isaiah 14:12-17...How art thou fallen from heaven, O Lucifer, son of the morning! How art thou cut down to the ground, which didst weaken the nations! For thou hast said in thine heart, I will ascend into the heaven, I will exalt my throne above the stars of God: I will sit also upon the mount of the congregation, in the sides of the north: I will ascend above the heights of the clouds; I will be like the Most High. Yet thou shalt be brought down to hell, to the sides of the pit. They that see thee shall narrowly look upon thee, and consider thee, saying, Is this the man who made the earth to tremble, that did shake kingdoms, that made the world as a wilderness, and destroyed the cities thereof that opened not the house of his prisoners?

Jesus spoke of the fall of Satan in Luke 10:18. Again what happened? Lucifer compared himself with God Almighty. He was not satisfied with who he was but said within himself, I will be like the Most High. He wanted to be God. Lucifer also took one third of the heavenly host down with him. Revelation 12:3-4...And there appeared another wonder in heaven; and, behold, a great red dragon, having seven heads and ten horns, and seven crowns upon his heads. And his tail drew the third part of the stars of heaven and did cast them to the earth: and the dragon stood before the woman which was ready to be delivered, for to devour her child as soon as it was born.

Revelation 12:7-9...And there was war in heaven: Michael and his angels fought against the dragon; and the dragon fought and his angels. And prevailed not; neither was their place found anymore in heaven. And the great dragon was cast out, that old serpent, called the Devil, and Satan, which deceiveth the whole world; he was cast out into the earth, and his angels were cast out with him.

Satan and his angels were cast out into the earth. This is the origin of the Devil and his angels or demons. Demons are fallen angels and/or angelic beings who are now unembodied spirits. Some teach that some demons are relegated to walk the earth, so to speak, and other spirits greater in power operate from the air or the second heaven. Satan does have a structured hierarchy. Over the years along with the scriptures, God has given revelation to his servants by way of visions and dreams to look into the kingdom of darkness.

So we are to cast out devils. The scriptures states the agenda of Satan and his kingdom. The Lord Jesus says, John 10:10...The thief cometh not, but to steal, kill and destroy, I am come that they might have life, and that they might have it more abundantly. The Devil and his angels/demons have no other agenda but to steal, kill and destroy.

Remember Satan conducts organized warfare.

> Ephesians 6:12...For we wrestle not against flesh and blood, but against principalities, against powers, against the rulers of the darkness of this world, against spiritual wickedness in high places.

This is part of a kingdom structure. Satan's attacks are planned and strategic. Satan (Head of the kingdom of darkness), Principalities (Princes) Powers, Rulers of darkness of this world, Spiritual wickedness in high places, Lesser demons of all sorts. There are strongman spirits; a spirit who leads group of lesser demons. Leaders, captains and lieutenants (remember a structured kingdom). There are familiar spirits and generational spirits. Satan's kingdom is structured because it came from structure. Satan is not stupid, he is wicked.

Consider that fallen angels, before they fell, held a position and/or purpose in the Kingdom of God. Though they fell, in the kingdom of darkness each demon holds a position with an anti-christic purpose. The angel Gabriel is definitely a messenger of God. Luke 1:26...And in the sixth month the angel Gabriel was sent by God unto a city of Galilee, named Nazareth.

In scripture, 2 Corinthians 12:7, Paul writes concerning his thorn in the flesh as a messenger of Satan.

Demons with negative purposes and agendas.

Jewish legend and history offers this study on the hierarchy of angels. It also is taught that Dionysius the Areopagite, Acts 17:34, is credited with the first study on angeology and their hierarchy.

(1) Seraphims-Isaiah 6:2-3

(2) Cheribiums-Genesis 3:24

(3) Thrones-Colossians 1:16

(4) Dominion and Dominations-Colossians 1:16

(5) Powers/virtues-Ephesians 6:12

(6) Principalities-Colossians 1:16

(7) Archangels-1 Thessalonians 4:16/Jude 9

(8) Angels-Isaiah 63:9

Satan and his angels fell from a structured heaven, it makes sense that he has a similar structure in the kingdom of darkness. Demons have negative purposes and agendas.

Chapter 4
Interview With A Demon?

John 10:10...The thief cometh not
but to steal, to kill, and to destroy...

In Luke 8:26-40...While Jesus arrived in the
country of Gerasenes, he encounters a
demoniac who lived in the tombs, amongst the
tombs or simply, he lives in the grave yard.

The demoniac had supernatural strength because
of his demonized condition. Mark 5:4-5...For he
had been often bound with fetters and chains, and
the chains had been plucked asunder by him, and
the fetters broken in pieces: neither could any man
tame him. And always, night and day, he was in the
mountains, and in the tombs, crying, and cutting
himself with stones.

This demon is terrified by the presence of Jesus
and says the strangest thing...Mark 5:7 And cried
with a loud voice, and said, What have I to do with
thee, Jesus, thou Son of the Most High God?

Listen to what he said—I ADJURE THEE BY GOD, THAT THOU TORMENT ME NOT. This demon here appeals to God for mercy! Notice he did not appeal to his leader Satan for help. He appeals to the Highest Power, God Almighty.

Then Jesus ask him, Mark 5:9...What is thy name? And he answered, saying, My name is Legion: for we are many. Jesus did not ask the spirit because he did not know. Jesus knew who he was and how many there was, and he did this for the sake of his disciples. What I need to say here is I have seen a few people giving so called clinics and they are quick to want to ask the demon his name and his purpose. Although this course of action can serve a purpose from time to time, a lot of demons do like to talk. Many times demons will declare things that are true such as who Jesus was; but caution, don't put your trust in what a demon says. I know, you believe he is under the arrest of the Holy Ghost, again caution, and focus. For example one minister says to a demon; What is your name? And the spirit gave him a name. And then the minister said why are you here? And the demon gave a grand cause of why he was present in the person and his assignment. Remember.

John 10:10...The thief cometh not but to steal, to kill, and to destroy...

Satan is the master of deception and the author of confusion.

Years ago, my Pastor had books by a well known minister, active in casting out demons. In one of the last books written by this minister he gives an acknowledgment to a demon who furnished him with information about the kingdom of darkness. How unfortunate. Deception is the enemy's chief weapon. A demon may give it's name and/or it's purpose but their intent is the same...John 10:10 The thief cometh not but to steal, to kill and to destroy. The scripture declares in Psalms 121:2... My help cometh from the Lord, which made heaven and earth.

Many ministers want reputations of uniqueness and want to be the authority in certain areas of ministry. It is enough to be successful in casting out demons. Jesus rebukes the seventy when they returned and gave their enthusiastic report. Luke 10:17...And the seventy returned again with joy, saying, Lord even the devils are subject to us through thy name. Jesus rebukes and says, Luke 10:20...Notwith-standing, in this rejoice not, that the spirits are subject unto you, but rather rejoice, because your names are written in heaven. We are not here to play with demons, to torment demons, lock them up nor give railing accusations against them, but rather to obey and understand what the Word of God says about them and cast them out in the name of Jesus Christ.

Examine the archangel's behavior when confronting Satan.

Jude 9...Yet Michael, the archangel, when contending with the devil he disputed about the body of Moses, (durst) not bring against him a railing accusation, but said, The Lord rebuke thee.

If the Lord removed his hedge (his protection) from around us, the enemy would do to us what was done to Job in the Book of Job chapter 1. The devil stole from Job, killed his children and destroyed their homes and later afflicted Job's body with acute sickness. Demons have no other agenda.

Obey God's Word and cast out devils by faith in the name of JESUS.

Chapter 5
False Ministers

Mark 3:23, And he called them unto him and said unto them in parables, How can Satan cast out Satan?

In Mark 3:22-27...When Jesus was accused of casting out demons through the power of Belzebub, Jesus declared that...How can satan cast out satan? And if a kingdom be divided against itself, that kingdom cannot stand. And if a house be divided against itself, that kingdom cannot stand. And if Satan rise up against himself, and be divided, he cannot stand, but hath an end.

Jesus is saying that the devil is not going to cast out the devil. Satan is not going to fight against himself. Christians should learn this lesson of warfare.

There are many con artists and those in the occult that advertise themselves as those that have spiritual abilities to cure spiritual ailments. No witch, no white witch, black witch, sorcerer, soothsayer nor psychic is coming against the kingdom of darkness. If they say they are good they are a liar.

Many desperate people were deceived through the television psychics and other palm readers. Thank God much of that has been put off the air ways. Presently there are so called prophets that are operating dangerously close to the psychic and/or demonic medium. It's all for money. They are charging large sums of money for people to talk to the master prophets. There is an observation of this practice, it is nothing new. 2 Peter 2:15...Which have forsaken the right way, and are gone astray, following the way of Balaam the son of Bosor, who loved the wages of unrighteousness. They have gone after the way of Balaam, prophesy- ing for money. That is not God's way. It does not matter what you know if it is not ministered in love, honestly and in the Holy Ghost.

There are no good witches, no good ghost nor poltergeist. If you are not serving God, you are serving the devil. There is no middle ground.

All through the scriptures, the adversary had demonic signs and wonders, witnessed by God's people.

In Exodus 7:9-12, the Lord told Moses to go before Pharaoh and to have Aaron cast down his rod. He

said it would turn into a serpent. Aaron cast down
the rod and it turned into a serpent. (1) Pharaoh
called for his magicians; they cast down their
rods and their rods turned into serpents also,
but Aaron's rod swallowed the magicians rods.

Moses was told to smote the waters and the waters
would be turned to blood. Exodus 7:19-25...Moses
and Aaron did so...in the sight of Pharaoh...his
servants, and all the waters that were in the river
were turned to blood. (2) Verse 22...The magicians...
did so with their enchantments: and Pharoah's heart
was hardened. (3) They also brought frogs up
upon the land. Understand the magicians power
brought only bondage and misery to Egypt,
because people believed a lie and an evil power.

But the magician's deeds faltered and they told
Pharaoh they could no longer contend; Exodus 8:19
declares that the plague was the finger of God.
Cheap magic and deceitful lies will only bring
bondage then destruction.

Acts 8:5-13...Remember how Simon the sorcerer
was said to be the great power of God, Acts 8:10.
Was Simon casting out devils? No, he was not. Was
he healing the sick? No, he was not. Was he getting
people filled with the Holy Ghost? No, he was not.
Yet, he had bewitched the whole city. I'll say again

there are some people who have gone after the way of Balaam and are prophesying for money. I pray they repent and come back on course.

A few years back some preachers got caught up in some cheap and shabby tricks; trying to give the appearance of the power of God. Again it's not needed neither is it wanted. Don't play with this. Ministry is serious. Again, many times when there's a great move of God, imitators and liars show up trying to duplicate and imitate. Most are trying to get a reputation, like the sons of Sceva. The sons of Sceva were PK's. They were the Preacher's Kids. It's not about us. It's about the Lord! These men lacked understanding and the Holy Ghost.

Acts 19:11,12...And God wrought special miracles by the hands of Paul. So that from his body were brought unto the sick handkerchiefs or aprons, and the diseases departed from them, and the evil spirits went out of them.

The disciples of John the Baptist received the Holy Ghost, Acts 19:1-7. Paul preached the Kingdom of God, Acts 19:8-10. God worked special miracles by the hands of Paul, Acts 19:11-12.

We are still talking about Casting Out Devils, Jesus Christ and the Kingdom of God. God exposed the fakers and liars when they showed up.

Spiritual Warfare

Acts 19:13-17...Then certain of the vagabond Jews, exorcists, took upon them to call over them who had evil spirits the name of the Lord Jesus, saying, we adjure you by Jesus, whom Paul preacheth.

14-And there were seven sons of one Sceva, a Jew, and chief of the priests, which did so.

15-And the evil spirit answered and said, Jesus I know, and Paul I know, but who are ye?

16-And the man in whom the evil spirit was leaped on them and overcame them, and prevailed against them, so that they fled out of that house naked and wounded.

17-And this was known to all the Jews and Greeks also dwelling at Ephesus; and fear fell on them all, and the name of the Lord Jesus was magnified.

18-And many that believed came, and confessed, and showed their deeds.

19-Many of those also which used curious arts brought their books together, and burned them before all men; and they counted the price of them, and found it fifty thousand pieces of silver.

20-So mightily grew the word of God, and prevailed.

Look what prevailed: THE WORD OF GOD.
Mark 16:17...In my name shall they cast out devils.
Isaiah 55:11...So shall my word be that goeth forth
out of my mouth: it shall not return unto me void,
but it shall accomplish that which I please, and it
shall prosper in the thing whereto I sent it. A great
revival took place after the devil was defeated.
The Kingdom of God was advanced and many
were saved and set free.

Matthew 16:18...Jesus declared...Upon this rock
I will build my church: and the gates of Hell shall
not prevail against it. The devil won't defeat the
purposes of God!

Chapter 6
Armed for Battle-the Armor

Ephesians 6:10-11...Finally my brethren,
be strong in the Lord, and in the power of
his might. Put on the whole armor of
God, that ye may be able to stand
against the wiles of the devil.

Today, many that serve leaders are referred
to as "Armor Bearers". The term means
one who carries the armor of another. A shield
bearer. One that attends to another. We are each
responsible for putting on the Whole Armor of
God. The armor is Salvation, Truth, Righteousness,
Preparation of the Gospel of Peace, Faith, the Word
of God and Prayer.

Ephesians 6:10-11...Finally my brethren, be strong in
the Lord, and in the power of his might. Put on the
whole armor of God, that ye may be able to stand
against the wiles of the devil. The scripture tells
each of us to be strong in the Lord, and in the
power of his might. The scripture tells each of us
to put on the whole armor of God.

At the time of the first century church the world was ruled by the Roman Empire. Jerusalem was under the rule of Rome. Paul compares the Armor of God to the armor of a Roman soldier. Ephesians was written by Paul while he was in a Roman jail. Ephesians is included in what is called the Prison Epistles.

Paul spent much time in the company of Roman soldiers and was inspired by the Holy Ghost to write the Epistle to the Ephesian church. The Epistle to the Ephesian church is still fresh and powerful instruction for today's church. Put on the whole armor of God.

As David is about to fight Goliath, King Saul covers David with his armor. Sauls armor was heavy and carnal. It was not suited for the battle that David had to fight with Goliath. 1 Samuel 17:38-39...And Saul armed David with his armor, and he put an helmet of brass upon his head; also he armed him with a coat of mail. And David girded his sword upon his armor. David took them off. Verse 50... So David prevailed over the Philistine with a sling and a stone. David was strong in the Lord and in the power of his might.

2 Corinthians 10:4...The scripture declares...the weapons of our warfare are not carnal but mighty through God, to the pulling down of strongholds.

Ephesians 6:10-18...Finally my brethren, be strong in the Lord, and in the power of his might. Put on the whole armor of God, that ye may be able to stand against the wiles of the devil. The scripture tells each of us to be strong in the Lord, and in the power of his might. The scripture tells each of us to put on the whole armor of God.

Loins Girded With Truth—John 8:32...And ye shall know the truth, and the truth shall make you free. We are free to fight girded with truth. John 8:36...If the Son therefore shall make you free, ye shall be free indeed. The bondage of sin is lifted and we are free to make war in Jesus' name.

Breastplate of Righteousness—Isaiah 54:17... No weapon that is formed against thee shall prosper; and every tongue that shall rise against thee in judgement thou shalt condemn. This is the heritage of the servants of the Lord, and their righteousness is of me, saith the Lord. Isaiah 59:16...and his righteousness, it sustained him. Righteousness is God's eternal and infinite provision. He sustains us with his hand. John 10:28-30...And I give unto them eternal life; and they shall never perish, neither shall any man pluck them out of my hand. My Father, which gave them to me, is greater than all; and no man is able to pluck them out of my Father's hand. I and my Father are one.

Feet Shod/Sandals With Preparation of the Gospel of Peace—Romans 10:15...And how shall they preach, except they be sent? As it is written, How beautiful are the feet of them that preach the Gospel of Peace, and bring glad tidings of good things. Stay ever ready to Preach the Gospel! Acts 16:16-34...In jail; Paul, beaten and in pain, was not distracted by his situation. He readily preached Christ to the jailer who asked, 'what must I do to be saved?' The jailer and his whole house were baptized and were saved because Paul's feet were Shod with the Preparation of the Gospel of Peace.

Shield of Faith—Romans 10:17...So faith cometh by hearing, and hearing by the Word of God. Hebrews 10:38...Now the just shall live by Faith. Diligently seek him. Mark 16:17...And these signs shall follow them that believe (they that have faith and use it); in my name they shall cast out devils.

Hebrews 10:38...but if any man draw back, my soul shall have no pleasure in him. Hebrew 11:1...Now faith is the substance of things hoped for, the evidence of things not seen. Hebrews 11:6...But without faith it is impossible to please him; for he that cometh to God must believe that he is, and that he is a re-warder of them that diligently seek him. The Shield of Faith will repel the fiery darts/attacks of the wicked one. 1 Timothy 6:12...Fight the good fight of faith. The enemy will send arrows and darts of strong delusion.

Helmet of Salvation-The Helmet protects our spirit, soul, and head of the body. We are saved in Jesus Christ. Acts 4:12...Neither is there salvation in any other; for there is no other name (than the name of Jesus Christ)...whereby we must be saved. Salvation is our escape. Hebrews 2:3... How shall we escape, if we neglect so great a salvation. A warrior in battle must protect his head. The head must be preserved and protected with all costs. The cost for our preservation and protection was the life of Jesus Christ. Injury to the head could result in death and/or put the rest of the body out of commission. Praise God for our Salvation.

Sword of the Spirit which is the Word of God-Hebrew 4:12...For the Word of God is quick, (living) and powerful, and sharper than any two-edged sword, piercing even to the dividing asunder of soul and spirit, and of the joints and marrow, and is a discerner of the thoughts and intents of the heart. The Sword of the Spirit is an offensive and defensive weapon. It is a two edged sword that cuts in two directions. It defends and attacks. Luke 4:1-13...When the devil came to Jesus to tempt him, during his fast in the desert; Jesus quoted the word of God three times and the devil left him for a season. 2 Timothy 3:16...All scripture is given by inspiration of God, and is profitable for doctrine, for reproof, for correction, for instruction in righteousness. Verse 17... That the man of God may be perfect, thoroughly furnished unto all good works. We should mount an offensive and defensive battle with the Sword of the Spirit which is the Word of a God, by preaching it and living it. Use the Word to counter attack the enemy's attacks.

Prayer-The long range weapon, such as a spear. Prayer can hit the enemy around the world. It is like the new tech missiles used in the Desert Storm conflict. It can't been seen or detected. Prayer hits it's target in the Name of Jesus. There is no distance in prayer. We are called to War in Prayer.

Jesus gave a great example of the ministry of prayer; Luke 6:12...And it came to pass in those days, that he went out into a mountain to pray, and continued all night in prayer to God.

Daniel prayed always, 3 times a day, in season and out of season. He fasted and prayed. Daniel 6:10...he kneeled upon his knees three times a day, and prayed, and gave thanks before his God, as he did aforetime. In the 10th Chapter of Daniel, Daniel fasted and prayed for twenty-one days and we see the scene of Holy Angels warring against Unholy Angels in the heavens.

Anna's testimony bears repeating again. The prophetess Anna's testimony is Luke 2:36-38...And there was one Anna, a prophetess, the daughter of Phanuel, of the tribe of Asher: she was of a great age, and had lived with a husband seven years from her virginity; And she was a widow of about fourscore and four years, which departed not from the temple, but served God with fastings and prayers night and day. And she coming in that instant, gave thanks likewise unto the Lord, and spake of him to all those who looked for redemption in Jerusalem.

People would call these Prayer Warriors unbalanced, fanatical and Holier Than Thou today. They were simply sold out to God. When you decide that you want to serve God this way, you will lose friends, and close minister relationships. Family will become unduly concerned and critical.

These saints understood the power of prayer, the purpose of prayer and God's will for prayer. The entire church in the earth has to return to prayer now. There is a beckoning, a calling in the Holy Ghost for God's people to return to prayer. Luke 18:1...Men ought always pray and not to faint...

In Isaiah 59:17, the armor is called the garments of vengeance. ...and he put on the garments of vengeance for clothing and was clad with zeal as a cloak. This is speaking of the Spiritual Armor that the Lord Jesus had on.

This verse also speaks of another piece of essential armor and/or clothing. A Cloak of ZEAL. The Cloak of Zeal—Zeal is executing fervently and/or with passion. We are to make war passionately and fervently. We are to serve God fervently and passionately.

Deuteronomy 6:4-5...Hear, O Israel: The Lord our God is one Lord: And thou shalt love the Lord thy God with all thine heart, and with all thy soul, and with all thy might. Serve God passionately!

James speaks of praying zealously. James 5:16... The effectual fervent prayer of a righteous man availeth much.

Romans 12:11 tells us to be...Fervent in spirit; serving the Lord.

Acts 18:24-26...These verses describe a preacher named Apollos who was...mighty in the scriptures... instructed in the way of the Lord; and being fervent in the spirit, he spake and taught diligently the things of the Lord, knowing only the baptism of John, and he began to speak boldly...verse 28 says Apollos...mightily convinced the Jews, and that publicly, showing by the scriptures that Jesus was Christ. Apollos had zeal to serve God with his all, with his life.

Paul had great zeal, Acts 21:13...Then Paul answered, What mean ye to weep and to break mine heart? for I am ready, not to be bound only, but to die at Jerusalem for the name of the Lord Jesus. That's Zeal.

Christ showed his Cloak of Zeal when he died on the cross. Philippians 2:8...He humbled himself, and became obedient unto death, even the death of the cross. John 15:13...Greater love hath no man than this, that a man lay down his life for his friends. Isaiah 59:17...and was clad with Zeal as a cloak. Thank God for his passionate love.

HALLELUJAH!!

Spiritual Warfare

Chapter 7
What Happens When Demons Are Cast Out

Matthew 12:43...When the unclean spirit is gone out of a man, he walketh through dry places, seeking rest, and findeth none.

In Isaiah the Lord speaks of a fast. The Lord speaks of the purposes of this fast. It is the fast of His choosing.

Isaiah 58:6 Is not this the fast I have chosen?
- (1) to loose the bands of wickedness
- (2) to undo the heavy burdens
- (3) to let the oppressed go free
- (4) and that ye break every yoke

Isaiah 58:6 describes what takes place when demons are cast out. The grip, manipulation, domination and influence of the evil is broken. During the loosening there is a war of good and evil. There is the loosening of the Holy Ghost and the resisting of the demon spirit. Both are supernatural powers.

2 Corinthians 10:4...For the weapons of our warfare are not carnal, but mighty through God to the pulling down of strongholds.

This spiritual battle is waged within the personage of a human being. A person's makeup is of spirit, soul, and body.

This encounter can be likened unto any warring incident or a rescue. The struggle can be like two children pulling on a toy or two dogs pulling on the same bone. Each pulling to declare ownership. Maybe you have seen two football players fight over a fumbled ball. The struggle is intense. Each one wants to come away from that encounter with the ball. Each one wants ownership. Also imagine someone being freed from the bondage of crushed metal, the result of an automobile accident and they are trapped inside. The freeing of someone who is buried beneath the rubble of heavy debris of a collapsed building that fell during a earthquake.

The observed behavior of someone being set free can be startling, frightening, or traumatic to the unlearned. So at this time let us look at what was observed when demons were cast out of people. We cannot change this. This is what happened when the Lord cast out demons.

Spiritual Warfare

In the Gospel of Mark, the ninth chapter, there is recorded a very graphic and descriptive account of deliverance.

Mark 9:17...And one of the multitude answered and said, Master, I have brought unto thee my son, which hath a dumb spirit.

Mark 9:18...And wherever he taketh him, he teareth him: and he foameth, and gnasheth with his teeth, and pineth away, And I spoke to thy disciples, that they should cast him out; and they could not.

Mark 9:19...He answereth him, and saith, O faithless generation, how long shall I be with you? How long shall I suffer you? Bring him unto me.

Mark 9:20...And they brought him unto him: and when he saw him, straightway the spirit tore (convulsed) him; and he fell on the ground, and wallowed foaming.

Mark 9:21...And he asked his father, How long is it ago since this came unto him? And he said, of a child.

Mark 9:22...And oft'times it hath cast him into the fire, and into the waters, to destroy him: but if thou canst do anything, have compassion on us, and help us.

Mark 9:23...Jesus said unto him, If thou canst believe, all things are possible to him that believeth.

Mark 9:24...And straightway the father of the child cried out, and said with tears, Lord, I believe; help thou mine unbelief.

Mark 9:25...When Jesus saw that the people came running together, he rebuked the foul spirit, saying unto him, Thou dumb and deaf spirit, I charge thee, come out of him, and enter no more into him.

Mark 9:26...And the spirit cried, and rent him sore (greatly convulsed him), and came out of him; and he was as one dead, insomuch that many said, He is dead.

Mark 9:27...But Jesus took him by the hand, and lifted him up; and he arose.

Mark 9:28...And when he was come into the house, his disciples asked him privately, Why could not we cast him out?

Mark 9:29...And he said unto them, This kind can come forth by nothing, but by prayer and fasting.

Look again at what took place when the demon manifested:

(1)   dumb spirit-the boy could not speak

(2) the spirit took him or directed where
     he travelled

(3) the spirit teareth him

(4) the spirit caused the boy to foam at the
     mouth

(5) the spirit caused the boy to gnash his teeth

(6) the spirit caused the boy to pineth (waste)
     away or loose strength.

(7) the spirit convulsed the boy

(8) the spirit caused the boy to fall to the ground

(9) the spirit caused the boy to wallow on the
     ground

(10) the spirit cast the boy into the fire

(11) the spirit cast the boy into the water

(12) the spirit attempted to destroy the boy
     or kill him

(13) the deaf spirit caused the boy not to hear

(14) the spirit cried

(15) when the spirit came out of the boy he was
     like one dead

This spirit had been with this boy since he was a child, Mark 9:21. So the spirit had deep roots and an old grip on the man's son. Jesus said unto them this kind can come forth by nothing, but by prayer and fasting, Mark 9:29.

When demons are detected the demon(s) may cause the person to flee the presence of the anointing. Also, when demons come out of people there may be the coughing up of phlegm. The phlegm may be clear, white, green, brown, black along with other debris. I know of an account where a lady spit up black rocks at a noon day prayer service. When a demon comes out, the person may sneeze repeatedly, cough, and make strange noises, or resist violently.

One thing people in the 1st century church days had on people today is the recognition of demon spirits. Mark 9:17...Master I have brought unto thee my son, who hath a dumb spirit. Matthew 15:22... Have mercy on me, O Lord, Thou Son of David; my daughter is grievously vexed with a devil. Mark 1:27...What new doctrine is this? For with authority commandeth he even the unclean spirits, and they do obey him.

Today there is awareness, yet people think that demons are a joke, a hollywood creation or figment of the imagination. There is also very, very subtle acceptance of the devil, the occult, and the black arts. At a very recent trip to a local bookstore, I saw a voodoo doll with instructions and pins on how to torment your enemy. There are many books on introduction to witchcraft! The voodoo doll was commercially packaged like a harmless toy and the books on witchcraft were packaged in very enticing, sparkling book covers with nice graphics. Also in the bookstore, were miniature idols of false gods. The devil of the 21st century doesn't have horns and a pitchfork (he never has looked like this). He does not just carry an air of darkness but of light and has packaged himself as an alternative to Jesus Christ. He presents himself as a god of choice and as a power to be reckoned with.

In a TV show an attractive lady was cast a good witch with supernatural powers that she used to offset evil and to help her family. These types of shows weakened any barriers people might have had against witchcraft and caused us all to laugh and let down our defenses. Other shows have the witches calling on God. This is deception. Warfare is serious!

I have a concern about the new vocations of Gospel/Christian Magician and Gospel/Christian Comedian. I have personally witnessed two Gospel/Christian magicians who said all of their magical feats were by slight of hand. One act told

the Gospel Story. The other act was pure enter-
tainment. For a truth putting Christian or Gospel in
front of a vocation does not make it necessarily
make it Christian, Gospel or right. Of late I have
seen the Gospel Strippers, Gospel Male Dancers,
Christian Homosexual Bishops and everything else
and these people want to continue in sin, defy the
Holy Scriptures and be excepted. The Christian
Stripper said she attended church regularly and
that a couple of brothers from the church had
come to the club and got a lap dance. All through
the Bible magicians were opposed to the Kingdom
of God. Whores are sinners. There are no Christian
Magicians in scripture. Some times we push grace
wanting to serve God our own way and end up
offering up something to Him that resembles,
Cain's Offering.

The Gospel/Christian Comedian—We need laugh-
ter and the scripture records this. Proverbs 17:22...
A merry heart doeth good like a medicine: but a
broken spirit drieth the bones. We should be very,
very careful of what we laugh at and belittle.

I am offended because I hear The Gospel/Christian
Comedian joke about Communion. Communion is
one of the Sacerdotal Functions that dates back
to the Exodus, Exodus 12:12. The word declares...
When I see the blood, I will pass over you. It is
sacred. The Table is where I can confess my faults,

my sins and receive forgiveness for my sins. A place where I can receive my healing. So I can't joke about or belittle communion. I was supernaturally healed of asthma for over 40 years now.

I am offended because The Gospel/Christian Comedian jokes about the Tithe. The scripture say the tithe is holy. One reason it's holy is it belong to God. So I can't joke about the tithe. I will not joke about the word of God that says if I tithe, He will rebuke the devourer for my sake and my endeavors would prosper. So I can't joke about or belittle the Tithe.

I am offended because The Gospel/Christian Comedian jokes about my worship and my praise. In the scripture we are exhorted to praise the Lord. God inhabits the praises of His Saints. My worship is sincere, in Spirit and in Truth, for God to God, for who He is. My praise is sincere and personal, to God and for God, for all He has done. So, I can't joke about or belittle my praise or anyone's praise.

Be so careful not to degrade or belittle the things of God.

Again; Casting out Devils and Spiritual Warfare is not for the unlearned or the immature novice. This is the Lord's Work and Ministry. This is serious work. The disciples were taught by the Master about 3 and 1/2 years with on the job training and observation of Jesus Christ Casting Out Demons.

The Scriptures, our ministry experiences, and testimonies of those set free are the proof that casting out devils should be preached, taught and shared. When demons are cast out in the name of Jesus Christ the Kingdom of God has come!

Matthew 12:43...When the unclean spirit is gone out of a man, he walketh through dry places, seeking rest, and findeth none.

Matthew 12:44...Then he saith, I will return into my house from which I came out; and when he is come, he findeth it empty, swept and garnished.

Matthew 12:45...Then goeth he, and taketh with himself seven other spirits more wicked than himself, and they enter in and dwell there; and the last state of that man is worse than the first.

In Mark 9:25...Jesus rebukes the demons...Thou dumb and deaf spirit, I charge thee, come out of him, and enter no more into him. Jesus shut the door on re-entry for the demons.

In Mark 5:10-12...the demons requested that they be allowed to enter into the swine that they not have to leave the country. Jesus permitted them but when the demons entered the swine the whole

herd ran violently down a steep place into the sea...
and were choked in the sea. It seems these demons
ended up in dry places.

Dry Places are Habitations of nothing. Demons
enjoy the habitation of a human being and has
access to the lifestyle that person lives and may
influence it. The demon seeks rest and findeth
none when he is cast out. There is no rest in Dry
Places. Rest for a demon is in a Human House.
The person's body becomes the demon's house
and/or refuge. The demon expresses itself through
the human's body until the spirit is cast out.
Matthew 12:44...The demon says that he will return
to his house from which he came. When demons are
cast out they are not destroyed, they do not die.
Demons that are cast out seek other vessels of
refuge, animals or humans. The delivered person
must guard and maintain their deliverance. Maintain
deliverance with prayer, worship, the learning and
practice of God's word. Be Accountable.

Demons in higher rule seem to experience something different, a temporary dethroning when their
power is bound. Daniel 10:12-14...Then said he unto
me, Fear not, Daniel: for from the first day that thou
didst set thine heart to understand, and to chasten
thyself before thy God, thy words were heard, and
I am come for thy words. But the prince of the
kingdom of Persia withstood me one and twenty

days: but, lo, Michael, one of the chief princes, came to help me: and I remained there with the kings of Persia. Now I am come to make thee understand what shall befall thy people in the latter days: for yet the vision is for many days.

When the angel and Michael fought it caused a breakthrough and the angel was released to bring Daniel the message. Daniel 10:20...Then said he, Knowest thou wherefore I come unto thee? And now will I return to fight with the prince of Persia: and when I am gone forth, lo, the prince of Grecia shall come.

It follows that when the second world kingdom Medo-Persia is defeated the demonic prince of Persia leaves as the third worldly kingdom (Greece) takes it's rule with a new earthly ruler and a new satanic ruler (the Prince of Grecia). It makes me believe that the weakening of the prince of Persia in the heavenlies caused the defeat of the Prince of Persia in the earth because the principality spirit was bound by Michael. Whatever is bound on earth, shall be bound in Heaven. When power and principalities are bound in Heaven: many with-stood ministries shall go forth. We must recognize, identify, and attack. Daniel 10:21...But I will show thee that which is noted in the Scripture of truth: and there is none that holdeth with me in these things, but Michael your prince.

When people are delivered from demons, instructions should be given to them to live a life of discipline. Praise and Worship, prayer, and the study of God's word must be practiced. The person should establish accountability through counseling or a mentor. The person should guard their deliverance, because of Luke 11:24-26.

When demons are cast out, many times a person's behavior changes. Luke 8:35...Then they went out to see what was done; and came to Jesus, and found the man, out of whom the devils were departed, sitting at the feet of Jesus, clothed, and in his right mind; and they were afraid.

When demons are cast out revival takes place. Acts 8:6-8...And the people with one accord gave heed unto those things which Phillip spake, hearing and seeing the miracles which he did; for unclean spirits, crying with a loud voice, came out of many... And there was great joy in that city. Also see Acts 19:11-22.

When demons are cast out, many times people are healed. Luke 13:11-13...And, behold, there was a woman who had a spirit of infirmity 18 years, and was bowed together, and could in no wise lift up herself. And when Jesus saw her, he called her to him, and said unto her, Woman, thou art loosed

from thine infirmity. And he laid his hands on
her; and immediately she was made straight and
glorified God.

Spiritual Warfare

Chapter 8
The Healing Connection

Luke 13:11-13...he called her to him, and said unto her, Woman, thou art loosed from thine infirmity. And he laid his hands on her; and immediately she was made straight and glorified God.

When demons are cast out many times people are healed. Luke 13:11-13...And, behold, there was a woman who had a spirit of infirmity 18 years, and was bowed together, and could in no wise lift up herself. And when Jesus saw her, he called her to him, and said unto her, Woman, thou art loosed from thine infirmity. And he laid his hands on her; and immediately she was made straight and glorified God.

There are sicknesses caused by bad eating habits. There are diseases contracted through water, blood transfusions, exchange of body fluids, or through sex. There are injuries obtained through trauma. In it all, the devil is directly or what seems indirectly behind it. No, we are not paranoid. I do not believe everything is a demon.

In Job, the 1st and 2nd chapters we see that Job's sicknesses came from the devil. Job 2:7...So went Satan forth from the presence of the Lord, and smote Job with sore boils from the sole of his foot unto his crown.

There was a prophecy given by Howard Pitman in the seventies. He said that God had given him insight into the strategy room of the kingdom of darkness. There he saw a great demon that would be responsible for catastrophic diseases. These are diseases that have no scientific cure such as HIV, AIDS, Cancers and some others. This prophecy was given many years before HIV and AIDS became popular. Today, we see a strange epidemic of AIDS and other diseases.

In these days of "Germ Warfare" there are people who are used by the adversary who systematically spread diseases and design diseases for the harm of mankind. Wake up! This has already been proven and is not just some conspiracy propaganda. None of these illnesses are accidents. Those who benefit financially from research and development of cures prevent cures from entering the country. There has also been an attack on natural herbal remedies. The devil attacks our

health very strategically. There is spiritual wickedness in high places! The love of money is the root
of all evil.

Revelation 18:23...For thy merchants were the
great men of the earth; for by thy (pharmakia or
prescription drugs), sorceries, were all nations
deceived.

Sickness came into the world through sin when the
devil deceived Adam and Eve. Sickness is from the
devil. Healing is from the Lord.

Acts 10:38...God anointed Jesus of Nazareth with
the Holy Ghost and with power: who went about
doing good, and healing all that were oppressed
of the devil; for God was with him.

Isaiah 53:5...But he was wounded for our transgressions, he was bruised for our iniquities; the chas-
tisement of our peace was upon him; and with his
stripes we are healed.

Let us look again at some testimonies in the scriptures of healing through the casting out of devils.

Luke 13:11-13...And, behold, there was a woman who
had a spirit of infirmity 18 years, and was bowed
together, and could in no wise lift up herself.
And when Jesus saw her, he called her to him,
and said unto her, Woman, thou art loosed from

thine infirmity. And he laid his hands on her; and immediately she was made straight and glorified God.

Mark 9:14-29 and Luke 9:37-42...Please review these two accounts for a broader view of what took place. In the Mark account the demon has caused deafness and dumbness, the spirit tried to kill the boy and more. Jesus cast out the dumb and deaf spirits, Mark 9:25. Luke 9:42...And Jesus rebuked the unclean spirit, and healed the child, and delivered him again to his father.

Matthew 12:22...Then was brought unto him one possessed with a devil, blind, and dumb; and he healed him, insomuch that the blind and dumb both spoke and saw. This person could not speak and could not see. When the spirit was cast out the person spoke and saw. Miraculous healing took place.

We must seek God to minister deliverance to people who are in need. We need the gifts of the spirit, such as the discerning of spirits, the word of knowledge, the gifts of healing, the working of miracles, and faith to work in concert for healing and deliverance.

Testimony

In a service, a woman came for prayer who had suffered with asthma for a number of years. When I laid hands on her, demons began to scream and threw her to the floor. She bucked like a horse and the spirits violently shook her. In a few minutes she was set free as we cast out the demons in the name of Jesus Christ. She wrote weeks later. She had been examined by her doctor and he said she did not have asthma and was released from taking her medicine.

In the prisons, we have cast devils out of numerous people who suffered with epilepsy and seizures. One morning, two ladies came for healing from seizures. Both ladies said that they were on medication and still were having the seizures. I told them that it was caused by demon spirits. I told them that when we pray for them that they might start to convulse, but it would be the last time. When we laid hands on them both ladies fell to the floor and began to convulse greatly. We rebuked the demons in Jesus name and the demons came out. Some people at the prison called for the medical staff and by the time the medical staff got there, these ladies were set free in Jesus name. They came back to the services months later and testified that the seizures had stopped and they were released from taking their medicine.

Testimony

Another woman came for healing from arthritis. When I laid hands on her she shook and fell to the floor. When she got up her countenance was drastically changed. Some months later she reported to her pastor that she was completely healed and was not taking any pain medication.

At another prison service, many men had received the baptism of the Holy Ghost and deliverance. At the end of the service an inmate came for healing. He said that he had a skin condition that made him itch constantly. He said that the infirmary had given him ointments and medicine, but that he still had the skin condition and the itching. He was scratching as we talked. I told him it may be a spirit. He said please pray for me. People around us were talking and having fellowship. When I laid hands on him in Jesus name he went up into the air and landed about six feet from me. The brothers backed up. The spirit was shaking him violently. I said to the men come over here quickly, it's a demon. We continued to rebuke the demon in Jesus name and in a few minutes the man was set free. He lay still for a few minutes as one dead. When he got up he was rejoicing. The itching had stopped and he was healed. After his great healing and deliverance, the man readily accepted the Lord Jesus Christ and he received the Holy Ghost with the evidence of speaking in other tongues.

Through the casting out of demons many will be healed. AMEN!

Chapter 9
Satan's Final Curtain

Revelation 20:10...And the devil that deceived
them was cast into the lake of fire and
brimstone, where the beast and the false
prophet are, and shall be tormented
day and night forever and ever.

L et us examine the betrayal of Jesus Christ
Luke 22:2-3...And the chief priests and
scribes sought how they might kill him; for they
feared the people. Then entered Satan into Judas,
surnamed Iscariot, being of the number of the
twelve. And he went his way, and communed
with the chief priests and captains, how he might
betray him unto them. And they were glad, and
covenanted to give him money.

At the eating of the Passover Jesus makes a startling statement. Matthew 26: 21...Verily I say unto
you that one of you shall betray me. John 13:21...
Verily, verily, I say unto you that one of you shall
betray me. Mark 14:18-19...Jesus said, Verily I say

unto you, One of you which eateth with me shall betray me. Luke 22:21...But, behold, the hand of him that betrayeth me is with me on the table.

And they began to be sorrowful, and to say unto him one by one, Is it I? And another said, Is it I? Matthew 26:25...Then Judas, which betrayed him, answered and said, Master, is it I? He said unto him, Thou has said. John 13:26-27...Jesus answered, He it is, to whom I shall give a sop, when I have dipped it. And when he had dipped the sop, he gave it to Judas Iscariot, the son of Simon. And after the sop Satan entered into him. Then said Jesus unto him, That thou doest, do quickly.

What courage to know that the adversary is upon you to destroy you, and to continue in the mission God has sent you to fulfill and you are the only one that can do this thing. You must go to the cross and die for the sins of the world.

We are talking about casting out devils. Jesus knew that Satan was working in Judas, but he was not distracted from fulfilling his purpose.

Satan attempted to kill Jesus through Herod when he was about two years old: Matthew 2:16...Then Herod, when he saw that he was mocked of the wise men, was exceedingly wroth...and slew all the children that were in Bethlehem, and in all the coast, thereof from two years old and under...Herod had

Spiritual Warfare

inquired of the wise men to let him know the location of the birth of Christ previously to the wise men finding Jesus.

The devil tried to kill Jesus at the temptation: Matthew 4:5-6...Then the devil taketh him up into the holy city, and setteth him on a pinnacle of the temple, And saith unto him, If thou be the Son of God cast thyself down...and He said basically the scriptures say that the angels will rescue you.

Then the devil comes in to kill or have killed the Christ, the anointed of God, the Messiah. He uses the treasurer of the Lord, Judas Iscariot. A man who travelled with Jesus Christ who saw the miracles, the healings and the deliverances. Judas was also a minister also who healed the sick and cast out devils.

Remarkable; and the reason I am reviewing the betrayal of Jesus is that just before the Final Curtain of the devil, similar behavior is present in the people in the earth.

After Armageddon the Beast and the False Prophet (chief agents of the devil) are cast into the Lake of Fire and Brimstone. Satan is bound for one thousand years and Christ reigns upon the earth for one thousand years. Revelation 20:1... And I saw an angel come down from heaven, having the key of the bottomless pit and a great chain in his hand. And he laid hold on the dragon, that old serpent, which is the Devil, and Satan, and bound him a thousand years. And cast him into the bottomless pit, and shut him up, and set a seal upon him, that he should deceive the nations no more, till the thousand years should be fulfilled: and after that he must be loosed a little season.

Christ reigns upon the earth for one thousand years. Peace, long life, and prosperity; a never before seen time like this. People witness and live this life with Christ. Just like Judas. Then the devil is loosed for a season. These people have to make a choice. Revelation 20:7...And when the thousand years are expired, Satan shall be loosed out of his prison, And shall go and deceive the nations which are in the four quarters of the earth, Gog and Magog, to gather them together to battle; the number of whom is as the sand of the sea.

It is quite remarkable that what is about to happen in this time, happens. To think that these people that had this time and experience with Christ could be influenced to fight against the King of Kings, The Alpha and Omega, The Beginning and The End, The First and The Last. Satan is the master of deception and the author of confusion.

Revelation 20:9...And they went up on the breadth of the earth, and compassed the camp of the saints about, and the beloved city: and fire came down from God out of heaven, and devoured them. How dare they challenge God Almighty!

Revelation 20:10...And the devil that deceived them was cast into the lake of fire and brimstone, where the beast and the false prophet are, and shall be tormented day and night forever and ever.

This is the Final Curtain for the devil, demons and the "kingdom of darkness", and Hell. Just as God said.

And the final White Throne Judgement:

Revelation 20:13-15...And the sea gave up the dead which were in it; and death and hell delivered up the dead that were in them; and they were judged every man according to their works. And death and hell were cast into the lake of fire. This is the second death. And whosoever was not found written in the book of life was cast into the lake of fire.

All that transgressed against God. Those angelic beings who kept not their first estate and those who transgressed against God over the ages were judged according to their deeds, and were cast into the Lake of Fire.

This is truly the Eternal End for the devil and his angels and for those whose names were not found in the Book of Life.

Just As God Said It Would Be!

Isaiah 14:15-17...Yet thou shalt be brought down to hell, to the sides of the pit. They that see thee shall narrowly look upon thee, and consider thee, saying, Is this the man that made the earth to tremble, that did shake kingdoms; that made the world as a wilderness, and destroyed the cities thereof; that opened not the house of his prisoners?

Isaiah 66:22-24...For as the new heavens and the new earth, which I will make, shall remain before me, saith the Lord, so shall your seed and your name remain. And it shall come to pass, that from one new moon to another, and from one sabbath to another, shall all flesh come to worship before me, saith the Lord. And they shall go forth, and look upon the carcasses of the men that have transgressed against me: for their worm shall not die, neither shall their fire be quenched; and they shall be an abhorring unto all flesh.

The devil and demons are spirits, eternal beings, and they will spend Eternity in the Lake of Fire.

Man is a spirit, a being that will live forever somewhere. Those whose names are not found in the Book of Life will spend their lives in torment forever, in the Lake of Fire.

Jesus spoke these words, and the Apostles echoed the same message.

Luke 13:3 and 5...except ye repent, ye shall all likewise perish.

John 3:5...Except a man be born of water and spirit he cannot enter into the Kingdom of God.

Mark 16:16...He that believeth and is baptized shall be saved; but he that believeth not shall be damned.

Acts 2:38...Repent, and be baptized every one of you in the Name of Jesus Christ for the Remission of Sins, and ye shall receive the gift of the Holy Ghost. AMEN!

Spiritual Warfare

Chapter 10
Hell and the Lake of Fire

Revelation 20:13-15...And the sea gave up
the dead that were in it; and death and hell
delivered up the dead which were in them: and
they were judged every man according to their
works. And death and hell were cast into the
lake of fire. This is the second death. And
whosoever was not found written in the
book of life was cast into the lake of fire.

Many people deny the existence of Hell and
the Lake of Fire. Even theologians and
bible scholars argue the torment of hell, the purpose of hell and its very existence. There is too
much evidence in the scriptures to deny any of it.

Matthew 25:41...Follows a statement from God to
the accursed...Depart from me, ye cursed, into
everlasting fire, prepared for the devil and his
angels.

Hell is cast into the Lake of Fire. Revelation 20:14
And death and hell were cast into the lake of fire.

This is the second death. And whosoever was not found written in the book of life was cast into the lake of fire.

2 Peter 3:9...The Lord is not slack concerning his promise, as some men count slackness, but is longsuffering to us ward, not willing that any should perish, but that all should come to repentance.

God never intended for any human to go to hell and/or to the Lake of Fire. They that reject God will live in torment in Eternal Damnation with the devil and his angels.

In Mark 9:42-48...Hell is described as a place where the worm dieth not and the fire is not quenched.

Mark 9:47-48...And if thine eye offend thee, pluck it out: it is better for thee to enter into the kingdom of God with one eye, than having two eyes to be cast into hell fire: Where the worm dieth not, and the fire is not quenched.

In Luke 16:19-31 is the much disputed account of the rich man and Lazarus. Many bible scholars and theologians call this a parable. Many believe a parable is a fictitious story created (figurative or discourse) or designed to teach or make an analogy (a comparison). Whether or not this is a parable or not, the question remains:

Is there a Hell?
Is there a Lake of Fire?

Consider it and I'll tell you the answer.

YES, THERE IS A HELL!
YES, THERE IS A LAKE OF FIRE!

Luke 16:19 is never referred to as a parable except by theologians and bible scholars and if it is, why do parables have to be promoted as a fictional story Jesus came up with to teach a lesson. Hell is real and people are suffering there.

Luke 16:19...Jesus says, there was a certain rich man. This means for sure, there was a particular rich man that He is talking about. Luke 16:20...And there was a certain beggar, named Lazarus.

This means for sure there was a beggar whose name was Lazarus that He is talking about. The two men existed and exist. One with God, the other in Hell. Hell is real.

I am VERY sure that the Ever Present, All Knowing, All Powerful, Eternal, Infinite and All Wise God, the Lord God referred to an actual rich man and the certain beggar named Lazarus.

We have to accept the whole Bible. We can't just pick what we like and choose the parts that don't make us uncomfortable.

Enough of this "Seeker Sensitive Gospel". Like it or not. The word of God offends and convicts those who are in sin. The same word that will convict you and save you, and will judge you if you neglect its warning.

Luke 16:19...There was a certain rich man, who was clothed in purple and fine linen, and fared sumptuously every day.

Luke 16:20...And there was a certain beggar, named Lazarus, which was laid at his gate, full of sores,

Luke 16:21...And desiring to be fed with the crumbs which fell from the rich man's table: moreover, the dogs came and licked his sores.

Luke 16:22... And it came to pass, that the beggar died, and was carried by the angels into Abraham's bosom: the rich man also died, and was buried;

Luke 16:23...And in hell he lifted up his eyes, being in torments, and seeth Abraham afar off, and Lazarus in his bosom.

Luke 16:24...And he cried and said, Father Abraham, have mercy on me, and send Lazarus, that he may dip the tip of his finger in water, and cool my tongue; for I am tormented in this flame.

Luke 16:25...But Abraham said, Son, remember that thou in thy lifetime received good things, and like-wise Lazarus evil things: but now he is comforted, and thou are tormented.

Luke 16:26...And besides all this, between us and you there is a great gulf fixed, so that they which would pass from hence to you cannot; neither can they pass to us, that would come from there.

Luke 16:27...Then he said, I pray thee, therefore, father, that thou wouldest send him to my father's house:

Luke 16:28...For I have five brethren; that he may testify unto them, lest they also come into this place of torment.

Luke 16:29...Abraham saith unto him, They have Moses and the prophets; let them hear them.

Luke 16:30...And he said, Nay, father Abraham: but if one went unto them from the dead, they will repent.

Luke 16:31...And he said unto him, If they hear not Moses and the prophets, neither will they be persuaded, though one rose from the dead.
I know the above scripture to be true, Luke 16:31.
I know a Bishop who died and was pronounced Dead On Arrival. He was bagged and tagged and

sent to the morgue. He was dead for 45 minutes. When he came back to life and woke up in the morgue, he was interviewed by the on-duty physician. He was a pastor of a thriving church. You would think people would be getting saved from his testimony. Most chose not to believe him though he came back from the dead. In the scripture Luke 16:31, Abraham is saying, your brothers have the word of God. The Law is the first five books of the Bible. His brothers had the prophets, which is the Word of God. If they don't receive the word, neither will they receive the testimony of one who came back from the dead. People don't believe this preacher's testimony. This Bishop carries his death certificate in his wallet.

Hell is a place of torment. The Lake of Fire will burn forever and ever. Hell will be forever in the Lake of Fire. Hell has been called the Regions of the Damned.

Hell and/or this region is made out of several parts according to the scriptures. These are Hell, Lower Paradise (Abraham's Bosom), the Pit, Tartaros and the Lake of Fire, the final containment region of the aforementioned.

Hell-Known as Hades—the prison of the departed spirits of the lost, where the worms die not and the fire is not quenched, a place of torment.

Spiritual Warfare

Scripture references: Isaiah 5:14, Mark 9:42-48, Luke 16:19-31, Revelation 20:14.

Death-the separation of the spirit and soul from the physical body when the physical body dies. Spiritually death is the eternal separation of man from God through sin, after the rejection of God's word and eternal judgement.

Lower Paradise-(Abraham's Bosom)- Paradise (Para means beside and dise means formed around. Paradise was beside the hell of torment)—was the prison of the departed souls of God's people. There was joy and comfort there. After the resurrection of Jesus Christ these souls were freed from lower paradise region of Hell, freed from death and were resurrected. Matthew 27:52-53...And the graves were opened; and many bodies of the saints that slept arose, and came out of the graves after his (Jesus Christ) resurrection, and went into the holy city (Jerusalem) and appeared unto many. Reference Isaiah 5:14... Therefore hell hath enlarged herself, and opened her mouth without measure...This was after the resurrection of Jesus and the saints lower paradise/Abraham's Bosom was empty. Hell got bigger.

When Jesus testifies in Revelation 1:18, I am he that liveth, and was dead; and, behold, I am alive forevermore, Amen; and have the keys of hell and of death. Jesus opened the prison of hell and death setting his people free to be with him in heaven. Though God's people were not in torment, they were bound by death. Jesus was the resurrection. The resurrection and its property got up with Him.

Hell-"Everlasting Chains Under Darkness"-Tartaros—the prison of a group of angels that sinned, who: Kept not their first estate, but left their own habitation. (Study Genesis 6:4...for thought) One view holds that angels went in with human women and that the offsprings were giants, who were unable to reproduce. Scripture References Jude verse 6, 2 Peter 2:4.

The Pit—The pit is the prison of Satan when he is bound one thousand years. Revelation 20:1-3...And I saw an angel come down from heaven, having the key of the bottomless pit and a great chain in his hand. And he laid hold on the dragon, that old serpent, which is the Devil and Satan, and bound him a thousand years, and cast him into the bottomless pit, and shut him up, and set a seal upon him, that he should deceive the nations no more, till the thousand years should be fulfilled: and after that he must be loosed a little season. The pit in Jewish writings is a long, continuous cylindrical, entrance to the Hell and the other compartments that has no end and spins continuously. Scripture does support that it is bottomless or has no end. Bottomless infers a continual downward drop or direction.

Isaiah 14:15-17...Yet thou shalt be brought down into hell, to the sides of the pit. They that see thee shall narrowly look upon thee, and consider thee, saying, Is this the man that made the earth to tremble, that did shake kingdoms; that made the world as a wilderness, and destroyed the cities thereof; who opened not the house of his prisoners?

When people cast out devils they sometimes IN IGNORANCE say to the demon, go back to the pit from whence you came.

The devil does not live in Hell and demons do not come from the pit.

The Lake of Fire-Is the final destiny of Hell, Death, Satan and his angels, the Beast, the False Prophet and every man/women who is not found in the Book of Life.

Revelation 20:13-15...And the sea gave up the dead which were in it; and death and hell delivered up the dead which were in them: and they were judged every man according to their works. And death and hell were cast into the lake of fire. This is the second death. And whosoever was not found written in the Book of Life was cast into the Lake of Fire.

The verse, Matthew 25:41, Follows a statement from God to the accursed...Depart from me, ye cursed, into everlasting fire, prepared for the devil and his angels.

Revelation 20:10...And the devil that deceived them was cast into the lake of fire and brimstone, where the beast and the false prophet are, and shall be tormented day and night forever and ever.

Thank God for our Precious Salvation in Jesus Christ. (Remember these precious words.)

Luke 10:17...And the seventy returned again with joy, saying, Lord, even the devils are subject unto us through thy name.

Jesus rebukes and says, Luke 10:20 Notwithstanding in this rejoice not, that the spirits are subject unto you, but rather rejoice, because your names are written in heaven.

Vocabulary

(1)   angel-a celestial being created by God, that serves God with great abilities and power

(2)   archangel-a higher class of angel, Michael is called an archangel and a chief prince

(3)   demon-a fallen spirit in service to Satan

(4)   destroyer-a descriptive name of Satan

(5)   Devil-the diabolical one

(6)   expel-to drive out or away, to cast out with authority and power as in the name of Jesus Christ

(7)   Father of lies-Satan

(8)   Lucifer-the original name of the devil before he rebelled against God

(9)   power-ability and strength

(10) principalities-a high ranking demonic spirits in Scripture

(11) Satan-the name given or ascribed to the devil after he rebelled against God

(12) sickness-an infirmity and/or weakness that causes pain, suffering, discomfort and physical abnormality

(13) warfare-as we know it, the armed spiritual conflict between the Kingdom of God and the kingdom of darkness

Spiritual Warfare

Casting out Devils and Spiritual Warfare is not for the unlearned or the immature novice. This is the Lord's Work and Ministry. In review, let us look at the Essentials. Remember for development and maintenance of the Warfare Life Style the following are essential Armor and weapons:

(1)   Scriptural Salvation

(2)   Develop and Demonstrate Love

(3)   Develop and Demonstrate Faith

(4)   Knowledge and Practice of God's Word

(5)   Maintain a Consistent Prayer Life

(6)   Minister with Integrity

(7)   Have Humility

(8)   Be Armed For Battle

If these truths and practices are not available to you seek out associations of like minds. You need to be mentored and taught by someone who is current in the field of Spiritual Warfare and Casting Out Devils.

I can recommend Good Books, Seminars, and Practitioners of the Faith. Contact me at: warfareevangelist@yahoo.com

Bibliography
and suggested reading

(1) Angels Elect and Evil, C. Fred Dickason, Moody Press, ISBN 0-8024-0734-X

(2) Christ the Healer, F.F. Bosworth, Whitaker House, 2000, ISBN 0-88368-591-4

(3) Demonology and Deliverance Volume I, Lester Sumrall, Sumrall Publishing Company, ISBN 0-937580-64-3

(4) Demonology and Deliverance Volume II, Lester Sumrall, Sumrall Publishing Company, ISBN 0-937580-54-6

(5) Discover Your Gift, Charles Travis, Logos Christian College and Graduate School

(6) God's Generals, Roberts Liardon, Albury Publishing, 1996, ISBN 1-88008-947-5

(7) God's Order For The Local Church, Daryl Merrill, Published by Daryl Merrill

(8) Greater Works, Smith Wigglesworth, Whitaker House 1999, ISBN 0-88368-584-1

(9) Healing, Francis MacNutt, AveMaria Press, 1974 ISBN 9-780877-936763

(10) Healing for the 21st Century, Aaron D. Lewis, 2000, Whitaker House, ISBN 0-88368-653-8

Bibliography

(11) Holy Spirit Revivals, Charles Finney, 1999,
Whitaker House, ISBN 0-88368-565-5

(12) Mighty Manifestations, Reinhard Bonnke, Creation House,
1994, ISBN 0-88419-386-1

(13) Operating in the Power of the Spirit, Larry Keefauver,
Charima House, 1997, ISBN 0-88419-494-9

(14) Pigs In The Parlor, Frank and Ida Mae Hammond,
Impact Christian Books, 1973, ISBN 0-89228-027-1

(15) Possessing the Gates of the Enemy, Cindy Jacobs, Chosen
Books, A Division of Baker Books, ISBN 0-8007-9223-8

(16 Power From God, Charles Finney, Whitaker House, 1996,
ISBN 0-88368-631-7

(17) Power Healing, John Wimber and Kevin Springer,
Harper Collins Publishers, 1987, ISBN 0-06-069541-2

(18) Prayer Evangelism, Ed Silvoso, Regal Books, 2000,
ISBN 0-8397-2397-8

(19) Smith Wigglesworth, Roberts Liardon, 1996, Asbury
Publishing, ISBN 1-57778-024-8

(20) Spiritual Authority, Watchman Nee, Christian Fellowship
Publishers Inc, 1972, ISBN 0-935008-35-7

(21) Spiritual Warfare, Richard Ing, Whitaker House 1996
ISBN 0-88368-385-7

(22) Spiritual Warfare, Derek Prince, Whitaker House,1987
ISBN 0-88368-256-7

(23) Strategic Spiritual Warfare, Ray Beeson and
Patricia Holsey, Thomas Nelson 1995 ISBN 0-7852-7972-5

Spiritual Warfare

(24) Strongman's His Name, Jerry and Carol Robeson, 1994, Whitaker House ISBN 0-88368-601-5

(25) Strongman's His Name II, Jerry and Carol Robeson, 1994, Whitaker House, ISBN 0-88368-603-1

(26) Surprised By The Power Of The Spirit, Jack Deere, 1993, Zondervan Publishing House, ISBN 0-310-21127-1

(27) The Battle Plan: Strategies For Engaging In Spiritual Warfare, George Bloomer, 2003, Legacy Publishers International, ISBN 1-880809-17-6

(28) The Holy Spirit and His Gifts, Kenneth Hagin, 2nd Edition, 1996, Kenneth Hagin Ministries, ISBN 0-89276-085-0

(29) The Master Plan of Evangelism, Robert E. Coleman, 1993 Fleming H. Revell, ISBN)-8007-8624-6

(30) The Mighty Miracle Power of Jesus, Theodore Fitch, Published by Theodore Fitch (No ISBN available, Nor date)

(31) The Ministry Gifts, Kenneth Hagin, 1981, Published by Kenneth Hagin Ministries

(32) The New Proof Producers, Morris Cerullo, 1998, Morris Cerullo World Evangelism

(33) The Secret of His Power, Smith Wigglesworth, Albert Hibbert, 1982, Harrison House, Inc, ISBN 0-89274-211-9

(34) The Soul Winner, C.H. Spurgeon, Whitaker House, 1995 ISBN 0-88368-340-7

(35) They Shall Expell Demons, Derek Prince, Chosen Books/ Baker Book House Company, 1998, ISBN 0-8007-9260-2

(36) Time Is Running Out, Reinhard Bonnke, 1999, ISBN 0-8307-2466-4

Bibliography

Elder Stanley Smith

Elder Stanley Smith is an ordained Elder of the Gospel of Jesus Christ under the ministry of Apostle Ralph E. Green. Ralph E. Green's Ministry is a ministry of Demonstration of Power. Resembling the Acts of the Apostles, many souls are saved, sick bodies are healed and demons are cast out in the name of Jesus Christ!

Elder Stanley Smith has been married for 30 years to Dr. Shiral M. Smith and they have three children all serving in ministry. Shiral is a gifted speaker, singer, author and former Minister of Music at Free Gospel Deliverance Temple. She is gifted and is used in prophecy, healing and deliverance. She holds a Bachelors Degree in Music and Christian Education and a Doctorate in Sacred Music. Shiral currently serves as Youth Pastor at Free Gospel Deliverance Temple.

Elder Smith has worked in many capacities in the church—church administrator for over 21 years, building projects, real estate, media, printing, graphics and television productions, producing over 150 national television programs along with albums, cd's and related publishing to the Glory of God.

Biography

Elder Stanley Smith is a Certified Bible Instructor through Logos Bible College and Graduate School/Jacksonville, Florida/Dr. Charles Travis, President. Elder Smith was also privileged to teach at The Potter's Institute in Dallas, Texas for 3 years. Stanley also served on the Ministerial Board and Prison Ministry at the Potter's House.

Elder Smith has a Bachelors Degree in Religious Arts and a Masters Degree in Theological Studies.

Elder Stanley Smith lives ministry in revival and has constant expectation of Great Powerful Demonstrations of the Holy Ghost. He presently serves as a staff Elder, Pastor of Evangelism and Outreach, Registrar of Open Bible Institute and is the Director of Community Outreach and Development Corporation, a home missions outreach at Free Gospel Deliverance Temple.

Elder Smith and family currently reside in Maryland.

Special Thanks To...

Altheria Jones, Annette Singletary,
Rozelle Jones, and Barbara Cook

Calvin and Gloria Fitzgerald
Paris London

Meshel Butler, Vizion Graphics, LLC
Layout and Graphic Design

Made in the USA
Middletown, DE
13 October 2023

40718278R00104